The *Oxford English Programme* 3

John Seely

Frank Green

David Kitchen

Steve Barlow

Richard Bates

Steve Skidmore

Christopher Stubbs

Oxford University Press

Contents

PART A   Stories, poems, and projects

Matters of life and death

PART B Using words

Presentation

4

Part A

Stories, poems, and projects

Home and away

The stories and poems in this chapter explore ideas about being at home and being away from home. There are some suggestions for talking and writing after the separate items, and other activities on page 23.

These photographs have been selected to illustrate different aspects of the theme. Look at them carefully and then talk about what each of them suggests to you about this theme.

The quotations that follow have been chosen to match the illustrations. Which one do you think goes with each picture?

> All happy families resemble each other; each unhappy family is unhappy in its own way.
> *Leo Tolstoy*

> The happiest moments of my life have been the few which I have passed at home in the bosom of my family.   *Thomas Jefferson*

> A man travels the world over in search of what he needs and returns home to find it.
> *George Moore*

> The rich man's wealth is his strong city; the destruction of the poor is their poverty.
> *Book of Proverbs*

> . . .Our neighbour and our work farewell.
> *John Keble*

> . . .And often took leave, but was loath to depart.
> *Matthew Prior*

Home

Home is the place where the diseased world dies
  at the door,
where the floor and carpet are worn by familiar feet,
where you can close your eyes and nobody says
  you are blind.

Home is where you don't have to be polite and
  sing cane-sweet song to coat bitterness,
where familiarity accepts you in its security,
where you know that love still breathes somewhere,
where your wife and children keep the other half of you.

When the rain broadcasts the glass face of the fields
  and moves the tidemark of the canals,
when you do not know where to go,
home is where they never say 'no'.

The small cottage that sits cosily under the palms,
the atap, brown with time and age hangs to the field,
the complaining hinges and wet stairs,
home is you
and where you hope to die.

Mohamad Haji Salleh

Home is a secret to share with a sister and her promise that she will not tell anyone.

Home is a place where you can be yourself.

Home is washing up the dishes, washing up the dishes and washing up the dishes. . .

What about you?
Write your own *Is* poem about Home.

Freedom

Freedom is not
a helpless grasping
at a source of hurt
or an outpour of oneself
to fixed ends others started

Freedom is not
a hiding in the dust
of righteous indignation
or a merging with shadows

Freedom is not
a becoming the model
of destructive echoes
or a walking in the hands of ghosts

Freedom is not
a reframing of oneself
in the walls of the old prison
or a becoming the tyrants' chain

Freedom is not
excursions of energy
to nowhere
driven and controlled
by someone else's motivation

Freedom is
a letting go like trees grow
a native self unravelling
and adventure of a new
self because of oneself

James Berry

Freedom is not having everything,
Freedom is having what you need.

Freedom is not doing what you think you ought,
Freedom is doing what you feel is right.

What do you think?
Try to write your own *Is/Is not* poem about Freedom.

Enchanted alley

Leaving for school on mornings, I walked slowly through the busy parts of the town. The business places would all be opening then and smells of strange fragrance would fill the High Street. Inside the opening doors I would see clerks dusting, arranging, hanging things up, getting ready for the day's business. They looked cheerful and eager and they opened the doors very wide. Sometimes I stood up to watch them.

In places between the stores several little alleys ran off the High Street. Some were busy and some were not and there was one that was long and narrow and dark and very strange. Here, too, the shops would be opening as I passed and there would be bearded Indians in loincloths spreading rugs on the pavement. There would be Indian women also, with veils thrown over their shoulders, setting up their stalls and chatting in a strange sweet tongue. Often I stood, too, watching them, and taking in the fragrance of rugs and spices and onions and sweetmeats. And sometimes, suddenly remembering, I would hurry away for fear the school-bell had gone.

In class, long after I settled down, the thoughts of this alley would return to me. I would recall certain stalls and certain beards and certain flashing eyes, and even some of the rugs that had been rolled out. The Indian women, too, with bracelets around their ankles and around their sun-browned arms flashed to my mind.

I thought of them. I saw them again looking shyly at me from under the shadow of the stores, their veils half hiding their faces. In my mind I could almost picture them laughing together and talking in that strange sweet tongue. And mostly the day would be quite old before the spell of the alley wore off my mind.

One morning I was much too early for school. I passed the street-sweepers at work on Harris' Promenade and when I came to the High Street, only one or two shop doors were open. I walked slowly, looking at the quietness and noticing some of the alleys that ran away to the backs of fences and walls and distant streets. I looked at the names of these alleys. Some were very funny. And I walked on anxiously so I could look a little longer at the dark, funny street.

As I walked it struck me that I did not know the

name of that street. I laughed at myself. Always I had stood there looking along it and I did not know the name of it. As I drew near I kept my eyes on the wall of the corner shop. There was no sign on the wall. On getting there I looked at the other wall. There was a sign-plate upon it but the dust had gathered thickly there and whatever the sign said was hidden behind the dust.

I was disappointed. I looked along the alley which was only now beginning to get alive, and as the shop doors opened the enchantment of spice and onions and sweetmeats emerged. I looked at the wall again but there was nothing there to say what the street was called. Straining my eyes at the sign-plate I could make out a 'C' and an 'A' but farther along the dust had made one smooth surface of the plate and the wall.

'Stupes!' I said in disgust. I heard mild laughter, and as I looked before me I saw the man rolling out his rugs. There were two women beside him and they were talking together and they were laughing and I could see the women were pretending not to look at me. They were setting up a stall of sweetmeats and the man put down his rugs and took out something from a tray and put it into his mouth, looking back at me. Then they talked again in the strange tongue and laughed.

I stood there awhile. I knew they were talking about me. I was not afraid. I wanted to show them that I was not timid and that I would not run away. I moved a step or two nearer the wall. The smells rose up stronger now and they seemed to give the feelings of things splendoured and far away. I pretended I was looking at the wall but I stole glances at the merchants from the corners of my eyes. I watched the men in their loin-cloths and the garments of the women were full and many-coloured and very exciting. The women stole glances at me and smiled at each other and ate the sweetmeats they sold. The rug merchant spread out his rugs wide on the pavement and he looked at the beauty of their colours and seemed very proud. He, too, looked slyly at me.

I drew a little nearer because I was not afraid of them. There were many more stalls now under the stores. Some of the people turned off the High Street and came into this little alley and they bought little things from the merchants. The merchants held up the bales of cloth and matched them on to the people's clothes and I could see they were saying it looked very nice. I smiled at this and the man with the rugs saw me and smiled.

11

That made me brave. I thought of the word I knew in the strange tongue and when I remembered it I drew nearer.

'Salaam,' I said.

The rug merchant laughed aloud and the two women laughed aloud and I laughed, too. Then the merchant bowed low to me and replied, 'Salaam!'

This was very amusing for the two women. They talked together so I couldn't understand and then the fat one spoke.

'Wot wrang wid de warl?'

I was puzzled for a moment and then I said, 'Oh, it is the street sign. Dust cover it.'

'Street sign?' one said, and they covered their laughter with their veils.

'I can't read what street it is,' I said. 'What street this is?'

The rug merchant spoke to the women in the strange tongue and the three of them giggled and one of the women said, 'Every marning you stand up dey and you doe know what they carl here?'

'First time I come down here,' I said.

'Yes,' said the fat woman. Her face was big and friendly and she sat squat on the pavement. 'First time you wark down here but every morning you stop dey and watch we.'

I laughed. 'You see 'e laughing?' said the other. The rug merchant did not say anything but he was very much amused.

'What you call this street?' I said. I felt very brave because I knew they were friendly to me, and I looked at the stalls, and the smell of the sweetmeats was delicious. There was *barah*, too, and chutney and dry *channa*, and in the square tin there was the wet yellow *channa*, still hot, the steam curling up from it.

The man took time to put down his rugs and then he spoke to me. 'This,' he said, talking slowly and making actions with his arms, 'from up dey to up dey is Calcatta Street.' He was very pleased with his explanation. He had pointed from the High Street end of the alley to the other end that ran darkly into the distance. The whole street was very long and dusty, and in the concrete drain there was no water and the brown peel of onions blew about when there was a little wind.

Sometimes there was the smell of cloves in the air and sometimes the smell of oil-cloth, but where I stood the smell of the sweetmeats was strongest and most delicious.

He asked, 'You like Calcatta Street?'

'Yes,' I said.

The two women laughed coyly and looked from one to the other.

'I have to go,' I said, ' – school.'

'O you gwine to school?' the man said. He put down his rugs again. His loincloth was very tight around him. 'Well you could wark so,' he said, pointing away from the High Street end of the alley, 'and when you get up dey, turn so, and when you wark and wark, you'll meet the school.'

'Oh!' I said, surprised. 'I didn't know there was a way to school along this alley.'

'You see?' he said, very pleased with himself.

12

'Yes,' I said.

The two women looked at him smiling and they seemed very proud the way he explained. I moved off to go, holding my books under my arm.

The women looked at me and they smiled in a sad, friendly way. I looked at the chutney and *barah* and *channa* and suddenly something occurred to me. I felt in my pockets and then I opened my books and looked among the pages. I heard one of the women whisper – 'Taking, larning. . .' The other said, 'Aha. . .' and I did not hear the rest of what she said. Desperately I turned the books down and shook them and the penny fell out rolling on the pavement. I grabbed it and turned to the fat woman. For a moment I couldn't decide which, but the delicious smell of the yellow, wet channa softened my heart.

'A penny channa,' I said, 'wet.'

The woman bent over with the big spoon, took out a small paper bag, flapped it open, then crammed two or three spoonfuls of channa into it. Then she took up the pepper bottle.

'Pepper?'

'Yes,' I said, anxiously.

'Plenty?'

'Plenty.'

The fat woman laughed, pouring the pepper sauce with two or three pieces of red pepper skin falling on the channa.

'Good!' I said, licking my lips.

'You see?' said the other woman. She grinned widely, her gold teeth glittering in her mouth. 'You see 'e like plenty pepper?'

As I handed my penny I saw the long, brown fingers of the rug merchant stretching over my hand. He handed a penny to the fat lady.

'Keep you penny in you pocket,' he grinned at me, 'an look out, you go reach to school late.'

I was very grateful about the penny. I slipped it into my pocket.

'You could wark so,' the man said, pointing up Calcutta Street, 'and turn so, and you'll come down by the school.'

'Yes,' I said, hurrying off.

The street was alive with people now. There were many more merchants with rugs and many more stalls of sweetmeats and other things. I saw bales of bright cloth matched up to ladies' dresses and I heard the ladies laugh and say it was good. I walked fast through the crowd. There were women with saris calling out 'Ground-nuts! *Parata*!' and every here and there gramophones blared out Indian songs. I walked on with my heart full inside me. Sometimes I stood up to listen and then I walked on again. Then suddenly it came home to me it must be very late. The crowd was thick and the din spread right along Calcutta Street. I looked back to wave to my friends. They were far behind and the pavement was so crowded I could not see. I heard the car horns tooting and I knew that on the High Street it must be a jam session of traffic and people. It must be very late. I held my books in my hands, secured the paper bag of *channa* in my pocket, and with the warmth against my legs I ran pell-mell to school.

Michael Anthony

Dobbo gets lost

I'm just walking along aren't I? There's me, Ferret and Dredge and we're supposed to be with that Mr Hawksworth, everybody calls him Hawkeye. He's a right laugh, you can do owt you want with him.

Anyway there's me, Ferret and Dredge and we're in that Trafalgar Square, where they have that fountain. Course we're at back, so I says to Ferret, 'Hold on a minute,' and he says 'What for? Come on we'll get left behind.' I say 'Don't talk daft, I'm going to get one of them pigeons. I'm taking one home for our old feller.'

Course Ferret doesn't believe me does he. Just keeps walking don't he, with Dredge. Anyway I takes my jacket off and I starts following these pigeons. They're dead tame, you can get right up to them. Anyway, I gets up to this pigeon, it were only a young 'un, and I drops on it with my jacket. It didn't half flap. So I thinks to meself, all I've got to do now is find a box. Next minute there's this old woman and she's hitting me with a stick. Course, I gets up, pigeon flies off, there's pigeon muck all over my jacket and everything. She gives me a right mouthful, this old lass, reckons I'm cruel and all the lot, so I says to her, 'Listen, supergran, I wasn't hurting it, I were just taking it home for my dad. He likes pigeons.' Course, she reckons she can't tell a word I'm saying, says she's going to report me so I runs off. When I look round there's no sign of Ferret and Dredge, no sign of nobody in fact. So I just walks round for a bit, has a look at them lions and that fountain. It were filthy that fountain an' all, full of fag ends and beer cans, and all time I'm thinking, I'll bump into Ferret and Dredge any minute now.

Next thing this bloke comes up. I reckon he were a foreigner, he'd a track suit on anyroad and he says, 'You take picture me yes?' So I says, 'You what, father?' Then he gives me his camera. He's got a grin on and that so I reckons to walk off with it like, for a laugh. Next thing he starts shouting, 'Stopee, you theever, you theever.' All these people start looking so I goes back to him and I says 'I were only 'aving thi on forra laugh,' and he just keeps saying 'Give back camera me you theever.' So I gives it him and runs for it. Then I sees this copper so I nips across road, up these steps and into this great big place. I thinks to meself, I'll have a walk round here for ten minutes, keep out of the way a bit and then I'll go back out and see if I can find the bus and if I can't I'll ask somebody if they've seen owt of Ferret and Dredge.

Anyroad, this place, it's called The National Gallery. It reckons to be some sort of museum. Mind you, for me it were a con, 'cos there were hardly owt inside it. It's true. There's all these great massive rooms with nowt in 'em. Well one or two had a few chairs in and there were some pictures hung up but apart from that there were nothing. Aye and another thing they'd got guards in all the rooms. I don't know if they'd got tommy guns under their jackets or what.

Then I sees this notice, Cartoon by Leonardo, or someone, this way.

So I thinks well it'll pass ten minutes on and I like cartoons. So I goes in and it's another con job 'cos there's nowt there. It's just this little room with a lamp and this scruffy little drawing.

By now I'm thinking that my best bet's to get back to the bus. Then I can't remember where it is, I know it's near some shops. So I comes out of this gallery place and walks about a bit. Then I sees him, Hawkeye, stood at a crossing. Well I runs up behind him, puts my hands over his eyes and shouts, 'All right, Hawkeye, old bean!'

Well I were capped when she turns round and starts hitting me with her bag. It's not Hawkeye at all, no, it's this right posh woman, and she isn't half shouting and that. So I runs for it.

Dobbo gets even more lost. Then he meets a local standing by a map of the underground. . .

Dobbo: R8?
Frankie: Yer wot?
Dobbo: Or 8?
Frankie: Wochew Onabart?
Dobbo: Just bein' pally. Sithee. . .
Frankie: Course. Tube map, ennit?
Dobbo: Ar. Wheer am a?
Frankie: I'm sorry pal. You're not comin' froo at all.
Dobbo: Can tha tell mi (look: watch mi lips) ar ter get ter Hendon North.
Frankie: On de tyoob.
Dobbo: Ar. R8. But wheer is thi one?
Frankie: Darn the frog an. Bout hundred yards.
Dobbo: What thy on abart frogs?
Frankie: Wer? Frog an' toad – road. Gedit?
Dobbo: I'm lost.
Frankie: Why din't yer say so?

David Harmer, Ian McMillan, and Martyn Wiley

Telling the story

1 What impression have you got of Dobbo and the way he thinks and behaves? Make up another story about him getting into a scrape. Write the story in a dialect that is familiar to you. Choose a title of your own, or take one from this list:
    Dobbo at the match
    Dobbo abroad
    Dobbo and the lollipop lady.

2 Look at the script at the end of the story. Think about the problems 'foreigners' may have with your local dialect. Write a conversation between a person from your area, speaking the local dialect, and a 'foreigner' (speaking a different local dialect, if you know one, or Standard English).

The banana tree

Before you read

Read the first three lines of the story. Think about what they mean and what they may tell you about the story you are going to read. Write down your thoughts. Then read the rest of the story.

In the hours the hurricane stayed, its presence made everybody older. It made Mr Bass see that not only people and animals and certain valuables were of most importance to be saved.

From its very build-up the hurricane meant to show it was merciless, unstoppable, and with its might it changed landscapes.

All day the Jamaican sun didn't come out. Then, ten minutes before, there was a swift shower of rain that raced by and was gone like some urgent messenger-rush of wind. And, again, everything went back to that quiet, that unnatural quiet. It was as if trees crouched quietly in fear. As if, too, birds knew they should shut up. A thick and low black cloud had covered the sky and shadowed everywhere, and made it seem like night was coming on. And the cloud deepened. Its deepening spread more and more over the full stretch of the sea.

The doom-laden afternoon had the atmosphere of Judgement Day for everybody in all the districts about. Everybody knew the hour of disaster was near. Warnings printed in bold lettering had been put up at post offices, police stations, schoolyard entrances and in clear view on shop walls in village squares.

Carrying children and belongings, people hurried in files and in scattered groups, headed for the big, strong and safe community buildings. In Canerise Village, we headed for the schoolroom. Loaded with bags and cases, with bundles and lidded baskets, individuals carrying or leading an animal, parents shrieking for children to stay at their heels, we arrived there. And, looking round, anyone would think the whole of Canerise was here in this vast super barn of a noisy chattering schoolroom.

With violent gusts and squalls the storm broke. Great rushes, huge bulky rushes, of wind struck the building in heavy repeated thuds, shaking it over and over, and carrying on.

Families were huddled together on the floor. People sang, sitting on benches, desks, anywhere there was room. Some people knelt in loud prayer. Among the refugees' noises a goat bleated, a hen fluttered or cackled, a dog whined.

Mr Jetro Bass was sitting on a soap-box. His broad back leaned on the blackboard against the wall. Mrs Imogene Bass, largely pregnant, looked a midget beside him. Their children were sitting on the floor. The eldest boy, Gustus, sat farthest from his father. Altogether, the children's heads made seven different levels of height around the

parents. Mr Bass forced a reassuring smile. His toothbrush moustache moved about a bit as he said, 'The storm's bad, chil'run. Really bad. But it'll blow off. It'll spen' itself out. It'll kill itself.'

Except for Gustus, all the faces of the children turned up with subdued fear and looked at their father as he spoke.

'Das true wha' Pappy say,' Mrs Bass said. 'The good Lord wohn gi' we more than we can bear.'

Mr Bass looked at Gustus. He stretched fully through the sitting children and put a lumpy, blistery hand – though a huge hand – on the boy's head, almost covering it. The boy's clear brown eyes looked straight and unblinkingly into his father's face. 'Wha's the matter, bwoy?' his dad asked.

He shook his head. 'Nothin', Pappy.'

'Wha' mek you say "not'n"? I sure somet'in' bodder you, Gustus. You not a bwoy who fright'n easy. Is not the hurricane wha' bodder you? Tell Pappy.'

'Is nothin'.'

'You're a big bwoy now. Gustus – you nearly thirteen. You strong. You very useful fo' you' age. You good as mi right han'. I depen' on you. But this afternoon – earlier – in the rush, when we so well push to move befo' storm brok', you couldn' rememba a t'ing! Not one t'ing! Why so? Wha' on you' mind? You 'arbourin' t'ings from me, Gustus?'

Gustus opened his mouth to speak, but closed it again. He knew his father was proud of how well he had grown. To strengthen him he had always given him 'last milk' straight from the cow in the mornings. He was thankful. But to him his strength was only proven in the number of wickets he could take for his cricket team. The boy's lips trembled.

What's the good of tellin' when Pappy don' like cricket. He only get vex an' say it's Satan's game for idle hands! He twisted his head and looked away. 'I'm 'arbourin' nothin', Pappy.'

'Gustus. . .'

At that moment a man called, 'Mr Bass!' He came up quickly. 'Got a hymn-book Mr Bass? We want you to lead us singing.'

The people were sitting with bowed heads, humming a song. As the repressed singing grew louder and louder it sounded mournful in the room. Mr Bass shuffled, looking round as if he wished to back out of the suggestion. But his rich voice and singing-leadership were too famous. Mrs Bass already had the hymn-book in her hand and she pushed it on her husband. He took it, and began turning the leaves as he moved towards the centre of the room.

Immediately, Mr Bass was surrounded. He started with a resounding chant over the heads of everybody. 'Abide wid me, fast fall da eventide. . .' He joined the singing, but broke off to recite the other line. 'Da darkness deepen, Lord wid me abide. . .' Again, before the last long-drawn note faded from the deeply-stirred voices, Mr Bass intoned musically, 'When odder 'elpers fail, and comfats flee. . .'

In this manner he fired inspiration into the singing of hymn after hymn. The congregation swelled their throats and their mixed voices filled the room, pleading to heaven from the depths of their hearts. But the wind outside mocked viciously. It screamed. It whistled. It smashed everywhere up.

Mrs Bass had tightly closed her eyes, singing and swaying in the centre of the children who nestled round her. But Gustus was by himself. He had his elbows on his knees and his hands blocking his ears. He had his own worries.

What's the good of Pappy asking all those questions when he treat him so bad. He's the only one in the family without a pair of shoes! Because he's a big boy he dohn need anythin' an' must do all the work. He can't stay at school in the evenings an' play cricket because there's work to do at home. He can't have no outings with the other children because he has no shoes. An' now when he was to sell his bunch of bananas an' buy shoes so he can go out with his cricket team, the hurricane is going to blow it down.

It was true: the root of the banana was his 'navel string'. After his birth the umbilical cord was dressed with castor oil and sprinkled with nutmeg and buried, with the banana tree planted over it for him. When he was nine days old the Nana midwife had taken him out into the open for the first time. She had held the infant proudly and walked the twenty-five yards that separated the house from the kitchen, and at the back showed him his tree. ''Memba w'en you grow up,' her toothless mouth had said, 'it's you nable strings feedin' you tree, the same way it feed you from you mudder.'

Refuse from the kitchen made the plant flourish out of all proportion. But the rich soil around it was loose. Each time the tree gave a shoot, the bunch would be too heavy for the soil to support; so it crashed to the ground, crushing the tender fruit. This time, determined that his bananas must reach the market, Gustus had supported his tree with eight props. And watching it night and morning it had become very close to him. Often he had seriously thought of moving his bed to its root.

Muffled cries, and the sound of blowing noses, now mixed with the singing. Delayed impact of the disaster was happening. Sobbing was everywhere. Quickly the atmosphere became sodden with the wave of weeping outbursts. Mrs Bass's pregnant belly heaved. Her younger children were upset and cried, 'Mammy, mammy, mammy. . .'

Realizing that his family, too, was overwhelmed by the surrounding calamity, Mr Bass bustled over to them. Because their respect for him bordered fear, his presence quietened all immediately. He looked round. 'Where's Gustus! Imogene. . .where's Gustus!'

'He was 'ere, Pappy,' she replied, drying her eyes. 'I dohn know when he get up.'

Briskly, Mr Bass began combing the schoolroom to find his boy. He asked; no one had seen Gustus. He called. There was no answer. He tottered, lifting his heavy boots over heads, fighting his way to the jalousie [shutter]. He opened it and his eyes gleamed up and down the road, but saw nothing of him. In despair Mr Bass gave one last thunderous shout: 'Gustus!' Only the wind sneered.

By this time Gustus was half-way on the mile journey to their house. The lone figure in the raging wind and shin-deep road-flood was tugging, snapping and pitching branches out of his path. His shirt was fluttering from his back like a boat-sail. And a leaf was fastened to his cheek. But the belligerent wind was merciless. It bellowed into his ears and drummed a deafening commotion. As he grimaced and covered his ears he was forcefully slapped against a coconut tree trunk that laid across the road.

When his eyes opened, his round face was turned up to a festered sky. Above the tormented trees a zinc sheet writhed, twisted and somersaulted in the tempestuous flurry. Leaves of all shapes and sizes were whirling and diving like attackers around the zinc sheet. As Gustus turned to get up, a bullet-drop of rain struck his temple. He shook his head, held grimly to the tree trunk and struggled to his feet.

Where the road was clear, he edged along the bank. Once, when the wind staggered him, he recovered with his legs wide apart. Angrily, he stretched out his hands with clenched fists and shouted: 'I almos' hol' you dat time. . . come solid like dat again an' we fight like man an' man!'

When Gustus approached the river he had to cross, it was flooded and blocked beyond recognition. Pressing his chest against the gritty road-bank the boy closed his weary eyes on the brink of the spating river. The wrecked footbridge had become the harbouring fort for all the debris, branches and monstrous tree-trunks which the river swept along its course. The river was still swelling. More accumulation arrived each moment, ramming and pressing the bridge. Under pressure it was cracking and shifting minutely towards a turbulent forty-foot fall.

Gustus had seen it! A feeling of dismay paralysed him, reminding him of his foolish venture. He scraped his cheek on the bank looking back. But how can he go back. He has no strength to go back. His house is nearer than the school. An' Pappy will only strap him for nothin'. . . for nothin'. . . no shoes, nothin' when the hurricane is gone.

With trembling fingers he tied up the remnants of his shirt. He made a bold step and the wind half-lifted him, ducking him in the muddy flood. He sank to his neck. Floating leaves, sticks, coconut husks, dead ratbats and all manner of feathered creatures and refuse surrounded him. Forest vines under the water entangled him. But he struggled desperately until he clung to the laden bridge, and climbed up among leafless branches.

His legs were bruised and bore deep scratches, but steadily he moved up on the slimy pile. He felt like a man at sea, in the heart of a storm, going up the mast of a ship. He rested his feet on a smooth log that stuck to the water-splashed heap like a black torso. As he strained up for another grip the torso came to life and leaped from under his feet. Swiftly sliding down, he grimly clutched some brambles.

The urgency of getting across became more frightening, and he gritted his teeth and dug his toes into the debris, climbing with maddened determination. But a hard gust of wind slammed the wreck, pinning him like a motionless lizard. For a minute the boy was stuck there, panting, swelling his naked ribs.

He stirred again and reached the top. He was sliding over a breadfruit limb when a flutter startled him. As he looked and saw the clean-head crow and glassy-eyed owl close together, there was a powerful jolt.

Gustus flung himself into the air and fell in the expanding water on the other side. When he surfaced, the river had dumped the entire wreckage into the gurgling gully. For once the wind helped. It blew him to land.

Gustus was in a daze when he reached his house. Mud and rotten leaves covered his head and face, and blood caked around a gash on his chin. He bent down, shielding himself behind a tree-stump whose white heart was a needly splinter; murdered by the wind.

He could hardly recognize his yard. The terrorized trees that stood were writhing in turmoil. Their thatched house had collapsed like an open umbrella that was given a heavy blow. He looked the other way and whispered, 'Is still dere! Dat's a miracle. . . Dat's a miracle.'

Dodging the wind, he staggered from tree to tree until he got to his own tormented banana tree. Gustus hugged the tree. 'My nable string!' he cried. 'My nable string! I know you would stan' up to it, I know you would.'

The bones of the tree's stalky leaves were broken, and the wind lifted them and harrassed them. And over Gustus's head the heavy fruit swayed and swayed. The props held the tree, but they were squeaking and slipping. And around the plant the roots stretched and trembled, gradually surfacing under loose earth.

20

With the rags of his wet shirt flying off his back, Gustus was down
busily on his knees, bracing, pushing, tightening the props. One by one
he was adjusting them until a heavy rush of wind knocked him to the
ground. A prop fell on him, but he scrambled to his feet and looked up
at the thirteen-hand bunch of bananas. 'My good tree,' he bawled, 'hol'
yo' fruit. . . keep it to yo' heart like a mudder savin' her baby! Dohn let
the wicked wind t'row you to the groun'. . . even if it t'row me to the
groun'. I will not leave you.'

But several attempts to replace the prop were futile. The force of the
wind against his weight was too much for him. He thought of a rope to
lash the tree to anything, but it was difficult to make his way into the
kitchen, which, separate from the house, was still standing. The
invisible hand of the wind tugged, pushed and forcefully restrained him.
He got down and crawled on his belly into the earth-floor kitchen. As he
showed himself with the rope, the wind tossed him, like washing on the
line, against his tree.

The boy was hurt! He looked crucified against the tree. The spike of
the wind was slightly withdrawn. He fell, folded on the ground. He lay
there unconscious. And the wind had no mercy for him. It shoved him,
poked him, and molested his clothes like muddy newspaper against the
tree.

21

As darkness began to move in rapidly, the wind grew more vicious and surged a mighty gust which struck the resisting kitchen. It was heaved to the ground in a rubbled pile. The brave wooden hut had been shielding the banana tree, but in its death-fall missed it by inches. The wind charged again and the soft tree gurgled – the fruit was torn from it and plunged to the ground.

The wind was less fierce when Mr Bass and a searching-party arrived with lanterns. Because the bridge was washed away, the hazardous roundabout journey had badly impeded them.

Talks about safety were mockery to the anxious father. Relentlessly he searched. In the darkness his great voice echoed everywhere, calling for his boy. He was wrenching and ripping through the house wreckage when suddenly he vaguely remembered how the boy had been fussing with the banana tree. Desperate, the man struggled from the ruins, flagging the lantern he carried.

The flickering light above his head showed Mr Bass the forlorn and pitiful banana tree. There it stood, shivering and twitching like a propped-up man with lacerated throat and dismembered head. Half of the damaged fruit rested on Gustus. The father hesitated. But when he saw a feeble wink of the boy's eyelids he flung himself to the ground. His bristly chin rubbed the child's face while his unsteady hand ran all over his body. 'My bwoy!' he murmured. 'Mi hurricane bwoy! The Good Lord save you. . . Why you do this? Why you do this?'

'I did wahn buy mi shoes, Pappy. I. . . I cahn go anywhere 'cause I have no shoes. . . I didn' go to school outing at the factory. I didn' go to Government House. I didn' go to Ol' Fort in town.'

Mr Bass sank into the dirt and stripped himself of his heavy boots. He was about lacing them to the boy's feet when the onlooking men prevented him. He tied the boots together and threw them over his shoulder.

Gustus's broken arm was strapped to his side as they carried him away. Mr Bass stroked his head and asked how he felt. Only then, grief swelled inside him and he wept.

James Berry

Enchanted alley

Thinking about the story

1 We see everything that happens through the eyes of a young boy. What impression do you get of him from the way he tells the story? Think about:

    age
    experience
    home background.

2 He is describing the area in which he lives, yet the particular place he is describing seems very strange to him. Why is this? (Look especially at the way he describes it on pages 10 and 11.)

3 How do the people of Calcutta Street react towards the boy? Why do you think this is?

4 What is the impression *you* get of Calcutta Street from reading the story?

Dialect

The people who live in Calcutta Street speak in a particular dialect. These are some of the things they say on page 12:

> 'Wot wrang wid de warl?'
> 'Every marning you stand up dey and you doe know what they carl here?'
> 'First time you wark down here but every morning you stop dey and watch we.'
> 'You see 'e laughing?'

1 Make a list of the other examples of their dialect in the story.

2 For each example explain what it means in your local dialect, or in Standard English.

The banana tree

Thinking about the story

1 **The Bass family**
   Go through the story again and find out all you can about the Bass family: how many of them there are, how old they are, where they live, what they are like as people, and how they get on with each other.

2 **The storm**
   Look at the way in which James Berry describes the storm at different stages:
   ● as it approaches
   ● when it first strikes
   ● as Gustus goes back to the house
   ● as he tries to save his banana tree
   ● as his father searches for him.

   How does the description of it differ at these stages?

   Why does the writer describe it in different ways at different points in the story?

3 **Gustus and his father**
   How does Mr Bass think of his son at the beginning of the story?

   How does Gustus feel about the way his father has treated him?

   Why does Mr Bass weep at the end of the story?

   How do you feel about the way in which Mr Bass has treated his son and how he now reacts to what has happened?

4 **The opening lines**
   Now that you have read the whole story think about the first three lines again. What do you now think they mean? Has your opinion changed since you first read and thought about them? If so, how and why?

5 **Symbols**
   This story is about a storm and a banana tree. But it is also about people and their feelings. To Gustus the banana tree is not just a plant. The storm, too, is not just violent weather. Think about this and describe what you think the storm and the banana tree stand for in the story.

Do you know the story. . .?

This chapter is about stories – most of them fairly unusual. There are suggestions for talking and writing after each item, and also on page 41.

Of course, if we hadn't stayed after school, we wouldn't have seen it. And if someone had tried to tell us such a story, we wouldn't have believed it, either...

When you don't have a brother or a sister, you get a lot of time to yourself and that is how it began...

It was the summer when the hot weather went on for almost three months. The level in the reservoir fell and fell, revealing more and more of the village that had once existed there. I had always imagined it as a peaceful place until...

You may think it's a strange thing to say that houses have personalities, but it's true. When I lived in that house at the top of Hangman's Hill, I found out for myself...

Everybody knew that Myra was a loner, and most people thought she was...well...a bit peculiar. But none of us knew that she possessed extra-ordinary powers until...

Make a story

There are five story openings and five pictures on these two pages. They have been paired off, but they don't have to be. Choose an opening, or a picture, or a combination of the two. Think of a story based on what you have chosen. Think carefully about what happens in it and how it ends.

Tell your partner

Now tell your partner just the last sentence of your story – don't explain your starting point, or what happens in the rest of the story. See if your partner can guess how the story starts and what happens in it. Then tell the whole story. When you have finished, swap over.

Blackbird

I didn't know what it was at first. He comes across the garden. Like we got these french windows and I could see him walking towards me – you know the way our Danny does. As if he owned the whole place. And there's something wrong with his mouth. It's like a big, black moustache. So I says, Danny what you got there. No, the cat. Danny's the cat. So when he comes up close I can see it's a bird. He's got this great bird in his mouth. And I hate that. He's always bringing me things. Moles, mice. He brought a squirrel once. Just laid it on the doorstep. It's like that every morning. It's littered with corpses. Like a sacrificial slab. And he looks so pleased. But I've never seen anything as big as this. I said, 'Oh Danny, you cruel thing.' Killing that poor blackbird. But it's not cruel is it. Not really. It's all they know, you know what I mean.

Then this thing, this blackbird moves. And I think Oh my God it's alive. That blackbird's still alive. And I hate things like that. I can't bear to touch it. All them bones and feathers. Turns me over. I said, 'Let it go, Danny!' I had to pull his jaws open. And you know what sharp teeth they've got. He didn't want to let go. And I can see this blackbird looking at me with his beady eye. It gave me the willies. Anyway in the end I got it out. I freed him. And he just lay there on the bread board. I opened the window so he could fly. But he wouldn't go. And Danny was prowling round making this terrible growling in his throat. I held it up. I said, come on kid, fly. But he weren't interested.

So I rings up Maisie. Said I've got a half dead blackbird here the cat's brought in, what shall I do. She said get it to fly. I said I've told it to fly but he's just not interested. She says it's probably shocked, how would you feel if a cat had carried you across the garden. I said he'd have a job. She says well keep it warm.

And Danny's nearly got it by this time. He's got this blood lust in his eye. I didn't know what to do. So I thought, I'll put him under the grill. Just keep it low, you know. Enough to warm him up. Well he just lay there. I didn't want to forget him. I didn't want to come back and find him roasted. So I set the timer in case I forgot.

So then our Harry comes home. He must have seen the light under the grill. He says, 'Something grilled tonight, is it?' I said, what. He said, 'Grilled chop is it?' I said, 'No, it's grilled blackbird Danny caught.'

He didn't believe me. But he looks under the grill and saw it was a blackbird. He gives me this look. He thinks I've gone mad. I told him what had happened. We did laugh. 'Course the bird didn't pull through. We buried it near the rhubarb. Well what else could you do?

Carole Senior

Pair work – reading aloud

This story sounds like someone talking. It is presented as if the narrator were telling the story to a friend.

On your own
1 Read it to yourself and try to hear this person's voice as you read.
2 Choose one paragraph to work on. Read this again and concentrate on hearing the storyteller's voice in your head.

In pairs
3 Now read your chosen paragraphs to each other.
4 Discuss what they sounded like: did each one sound like your idea of the storyteller?
5 Practise your readings again until you are both satisfied that you have captured the storyteller's voice.

Making up a comic strip

1 Think of an idea

Comic strip ideas can be original – made up by the writer

> Some criminals want to kidnap a famous and very rich film star. She is working on a film in which she plays the part of a police officer. They kidnap her, but when they get her back to their hideout they discover that they have kidnapped a real police officer.

– or they can be based on a story you have read (in this case a well known story that someone has adapted).

> When Sultan Aladdin lay dying, he sent for his two sons, Ringading and Gongalong. The brothers were very similar in looks and character, but they were always jealous of each other and so they never stopped quarrelling. Aladdin was afraid that once he was dead, the brothers would fight for power and so cause great suffering to the people.
>   'Now, listen carefully,' he said as they stood on either side of his bed.

2 Write a script

The next thing to do is to write the script. You will notice that this has two main parts:

What is in the pictures

What is in the speech bubbles, thought bubbles, and captions.

> Frame 1
> Picture: Sultan Aladdin lying back on a magnificent bed, surrounded by courtiers. The Sultan has just sent a messenger to fetch his sons.
> Caption: When Sultan Aladdin lay dying, he sent for his two sons.
>
> Frame 2
> Picture: a room in the Sultan's palace. There are two framed pictures on the wall. They show identical boys. Underneath there are labels: 'Ringading' and 'Gongalong.'
>
> Frame 3
> Picture: Ringading and Gongalong as young men. They are fighting.
> Caption: Ringading and Gongalong were always jealous of each other and so they never stopped quarrelling.
>
> Frame 4
> Picture: the two sons standing at the foot of the Sultan's bed. They are glaring at each other. The Sultan is speaking.
> Speech bubble: Now listen carefully...

3 Draw the strip

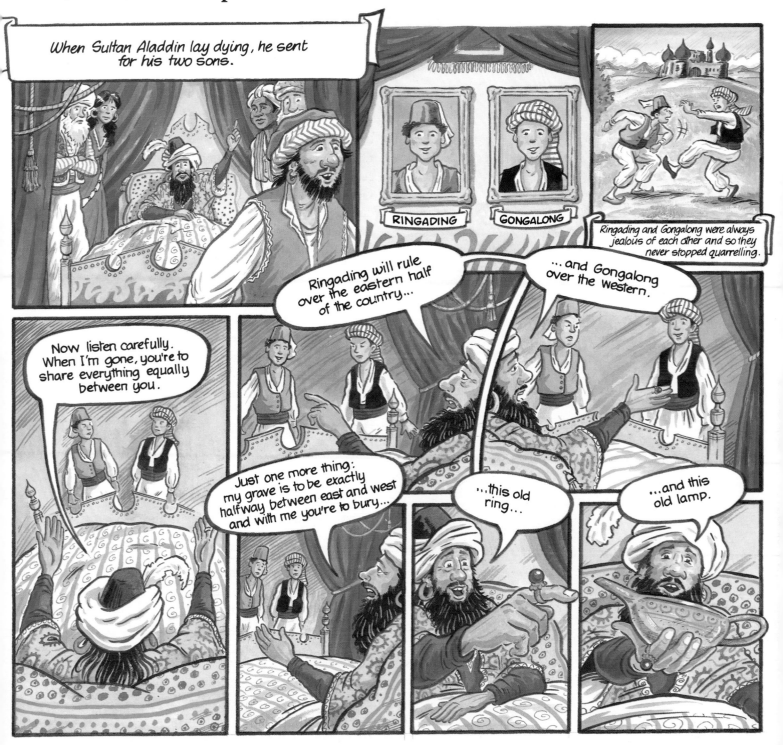

1 Look at the comic strip on this page. The script for the first four frames is printed opposite. Write the script for the remaining five frames.

2 Look at the story idea about the kidnappers at the top of the opposite page. Think of how it might start. Write the script for the first four frames. When you have done that, draw them.

3 Now tackle a full story. Follow the instructions on these two pages and make up your own comic strip. You could work:
- on your own (difficult, but rewarding if it works)
- with a partner (good if one of you can draw and the other write the script)
- in a group (quick, if you can agree on things).

The galloping cat

Oh I am a cat that likes to
Gallop about doing good
So
One day when I was
Galloping about doing good, I saw
A figure in the path; I said:
Get off! (Be-
cause
I am a cat that likes to
Gallop about doing good)
But he did not move, instead
He raised his hand as if
To land me a cuff
So I made to dodge so as to
Prevent him bring it orf,
Un-for-tune-ately I slid
On a banana skin
Some ass had left instead
Of putting in the bin. So
His hand caught me on the cheek
I tried
To lay his arm open from wrist to elbow
With my sharp teeth
Because I am
A cat that likes to gallop about doing good
Would you believe it?
He wasn't there
My teeth met nothing but air,
But a Voice said: Poor cat,
(Meaning me) and a soft stroke
Came on me head
Since when
I have been bald.

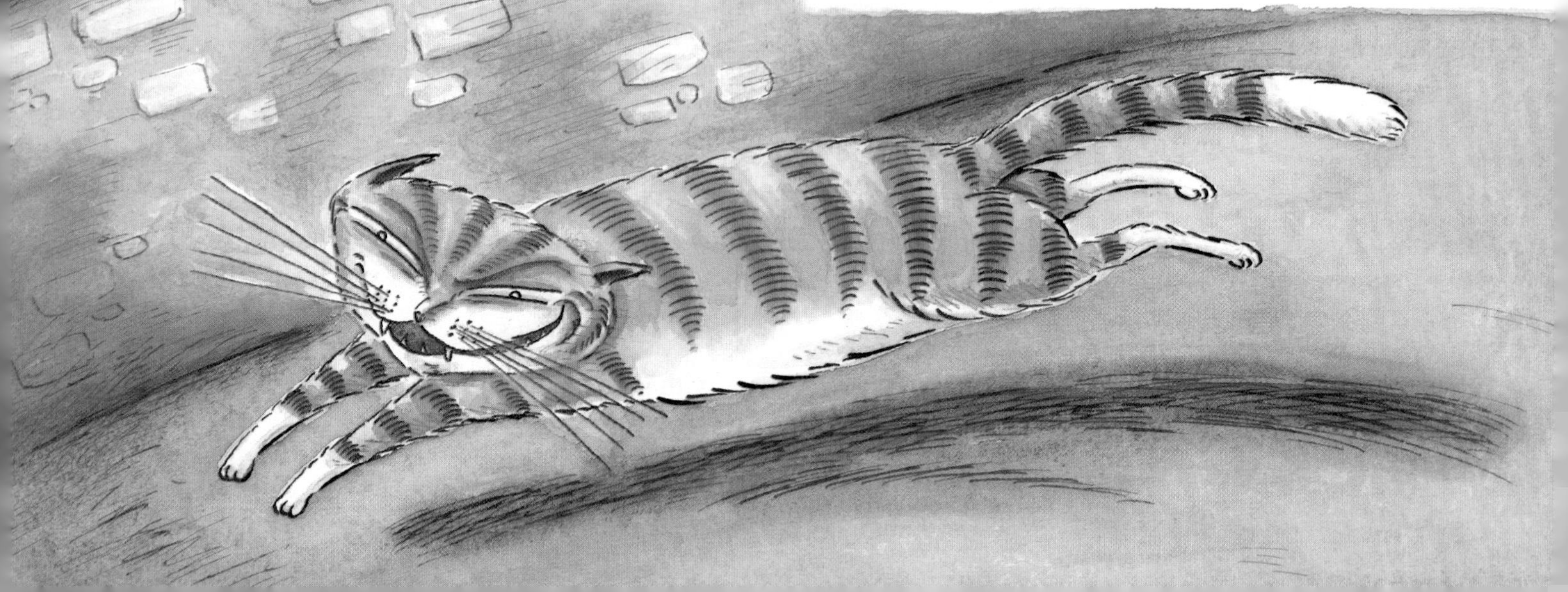

I regard myself as
A martyr to doing good.
Also I heard a swoosh
As of wings, and saw
A halo shining at the height of
Mrs Gubbins's backyard fence,
So I thought: What's the good
Of galloping about doing good
When angels stand in the path
And do not do as they should
Such as having an arm to be bitten off
All the same I
Intend to go on being
A cat that likes to
Gallop about doing good
So
Now with my bald head I go,
Chopping the untidy flowers down, to and fro,
An' scooping up the grass to show
Underneath
The cinder path of wrath
Ha ha ha ha, ho,
Angels aren't the only ones who do not know
What's what and that
Galloping about doing good
Is a full-time job
That needs
An experienced eye of earthly
Sharpness, worth I dare say
(If you'll forgive a personal note)
A good deal more
Than all that skyey stuff
Of angels that make so bold as
To pity a cat like me that
Gallops about doing good.

Stevie Smith

Further adventures of the galloping cat

Think of other things that might happen to this
cat and describe another of its adventures.
For example:
> The galloping cat and the clumsy burglar
> The galloping cat and the new neighbours
> The galloping cat and the man from the
> RSPCA.

As you write the story, try to capture the cat's
tone of voice.

Welsh incident

'But that was nothing to what things came out
From the sea-caves of Criccieth yonder.'
'What were they? Mermaids? dragons? ghosts?'
'Nothing at all of any things like that.'
'What were they, then?'
                        'All sorts of queer things,
Things never seen or heard or written about,
Very strange, un-Welsh, utterly peculiar
Things. Oh, solid enough they seemed to touch,
Had anyone dared it. Marvellous creation,
All various shapes and sizes and no sizes,
All new, each perfectly unlike his neighbour,
Though all came moving slowly out together.'
'Describe just one of them.'
                              'I am unable.'
'What were their colours?'
                          'Mostly nameless colours,
Colours you'd like to see; but one was puce
Or perhaps more like crimson, but not purplish.
Some had no colour.'
                    'Tell me, had they legs?'
'Not a leg nor foot among them that I saw.'
'But did these things come out in any order?
What o'clock was it? What was the day of the week?
Who else was present? How was the weather?'

'I was coming to that. It was half-past three
On Easter Tuesday last. The sun was shining.
The Harlech Silver Band played *Marchog Jesu*
On thirty-seven shimmering instruments,
Collecting for Carnarvon's (Fever) Hospital Fund.
The populations of Pwllheli, Criccieth,
Portmadoc, Borth, Tremadoc, Penrhyndeudraeth,
Were all assembled. Criccieth's mayor addressed them
First in good Welsh and then in fluent English,
Twisting his fingers in his chain of office,
Welcoming the things. They came out on the sand,
Not keeping time to the band, moving seaward
Silently at a snail's pace. But at last
The most odd, indescribable thing of all
Which hardly one man there could see for wonder
Did something recognizably a something.'
'Well, what?'
       'It made a noise.'
            'A frightening noise?'
'No, no.'
     'A musical noise? A noise of scuffling?'
'No, but a very loud, respectable noise –
Like groaning to oneself on Sunday morning
In Chapel, close before the second psalm.'
'What did the mayor do?'
         'I was coming to that.'

Robert Graves

Newspaper report

Suppose that the concert given by the Harlech Silver Band was attended by a reporter from the local newspaper. She witnessed everything that happened. The story was front page news. Write the full report in which she describes what she saw.

The story continues

The poem ends with the speaker in the middle of the story:

'What did the mayor do?'
         'I was coming to that.'

But we never discover what the mayor did. Think about how the conversation might have continued and ended. Write your own continuation. You may, if you like, reveal what the creatures were, or you may keep it a secret as the poem does.

The pishogue

Without warning it tore in from the south-east – a mean, black,
murderous storm that pounced on our fishing fleet, driving the boats
before it, sails reefed down to the merest rags as they scuttled for the
shelter of Sheephaven dock. For a day and a night the wind did its worst
to us, resentful that anything could escape its fury. It seemed to me – a
youngster just starting school – that all the waves of the world, a mad
tormented host, were being rounded up and driven down on us in a
terrified stampede – huge bull-like waves that charged bellowing with
lowered crests; monsters that reared their green bulk high over the sea
wall to stamp their foaming hoofs on the boats not yet hauled up to
safety; as far out as the eye could see an ocean of plunging waves with
overhead a whirling curtain of mist – the sweat from their steaming
flanks.

That night I woke with a queer sensation of just-having-missed-hearing-
something. Not the storm which still howled round the house, but
something unfamiliar and much more important. Tense and expectant I
waited for the sound to be repeated. At last it came – from far out to sea –
a high, wailing, human scream muted by the storm but still clear and
distinct. It could have been the cry of a curlew or a solitary homing sea-
gull, there was in it such an awful desolation of loneliness and futility.
For what seemed ages there was nothing to be heard but the wind and the

sea and the clawing gusts of rain on the window. Then it came again, urgent and shrill with terror, voicing its bitter protest – a poor lost thing, naked and shivering and doomed, that yet dared to bare its teeth at eternity. The next I knew was a gasping shout that must have been my own, candle-light dazzling my eyes and my mother sitting on the bed telling me it was all only a nightmare.

When I heard that the *Bessie Morgan* had been driven on the rocks during the night, I bolted my breakfast and raced down to the quay. I knew the *Bessie Morgan* well. A two-masted schooner of around one hundred tons, she was in the coal-carrying trade between Swansea and the south coast of Ireland. She had a crew of three – the skipper and owner, a grim taciturn man, seldom seen and always avoided; the mate, whom I can only remember as a burly figure forever pacing the deck, and Ginger, the deck-hand. Ginger was a friendly soul, cheerful as a cricket. Never have I known anyone so blatantly alive. He shouted and cursed and worked like a demon all day and at night swaggered off up the village to Jonty Gallagher's where he would drink pints of draught till it almost ran out of his eyes. Everybody liked him, even the old people. To me he was an immortal – a roistering, guzzling, benevolent demi-god.

Four or five times a year the *Bessie Morgan* put in to Sheephaven, spent about four days unloading and waddled off again in ballast like an enormous black duck. Though clumsy, she was stoutly built – squat and beamy, capable of weathering the worst that sea and wind could do to her.

Yet there she was, a couple of cable-lengths out to sea, crushed and broken on the rocks guarding the bay. She leaned over drunkenly on her port beam exposing a mangled deck from which everything had been swept away – ship's dinghy, ventilators, donkey-engine, hatches. Even the wheelhouse was gone. Of her after-mast there was only a jagged stump; her foremast, snapped off at man's height, trailed dejectedly in the sea, an unholy tangle of gear and tattered canvas preventing it from being washed away; her hold gaped open and from it a trickling saliva of coal and seawater streaked the deck at every lurch she gave. Her figure-head – a sooty full-breasted female – had been carried away along with the bowsprit, so I started off at once up the beach to look for it. For all I knew or cared the *Bessie Morgan*'s crew might still have been sleeping safe and sound in their bunks.

They found two bodies that day. The mate's washed up on Ballyvawn beach, Ginger's in a deep pool among the rocks farther up the coast. I was at the dock when they brought Ginger's body in – a sodden, swollen, inert heap stretched face downwards across the thwarts. Death, I had always thought, was something cold and impersonal and not at all frightening; it stretched out decently in bed, brown-shrouded and unfamiliar, on its features the smug waxen serenity of a holy picture; not a poor sea-ravaged thing, without manhood or dignity, its head lolling on the floorboards, the sea-water drooling from the gaping mouth.

One of the fishermen told me they found him kneeling down with his face buried in the sand – 'like he was praying'. For nights afterwards I used to dream of cool, green depths and a dark figure outlined against white sand, a figure that crouched on its hams, head bent and arms outflung, in an attitude of grotesque adoration.

A Sunday afternoon three weeks after the wreck. The sea nearly dead calm drowsing under a mild September sun. The beach dotted with knots of excited men and women, gabbling away sixteen to the dozen. A constant shifting and changing as people moved round from group to group gleaning information.

Scanty enough it was. Listening to Mick Donnelly holding forth to a few cronies, I had learnt all there was to know – an old priest living in retirement in the village had been persuaded to attempt the recovery of the skipper's body.

Mick, of course, poured scorn on the whole project, but then with Mick, disbelief was a matter of principle. A lifetime of argument and contrariness had turned him into a fanatical sceptic. He sat now, a sour-faced, thin-lipped little runt of a man, hunched up on a rock moodily eyeing the crowd.

'Pishogues!' he snorted contemptuously. 'Them and their bloody pishogues! It's bad enough for crazy ould faggots of women to be mixin' muggard and slaughterin' cocks on Martin's night and buryin' hoofs and hen eggs in their neighbours' fields, but to be draggin' poor Father Brady down here on an errand of the sort' – he paused and shook his head sorrowfully – 'it's not Christian.'

A shocked chorus of protest broke out. 'Go aisy now, Mick.' 'Sure Father Brady wouldn't have dealings with the like.' 'Take care how ye insult the cloth.'

'What's pishogues?' I inquired timidly.

Mick ignored me. 'I'm not sayin' one word against Father Brady,' he resumed. 'No more he's off the mission these ten years and must be goin' on ninety now. No! I'll tell ye who's at the back of all this. It's the same ignorant gulpins who've been goin' round preachin' that as long as a drowned man stops in the water there'll be no luck in the fishin'. Better for us if the whole bloody coast were alive with corpses – there'd be a run of mackerel to beat the band. And now these prime boys think they've got some pishogue that'll bring the body leppin' up out of the water like a trout. Mark my words. . .' He broke off suddenly and pointed up the beach.

'Here he comes now, lads,' he exclaimed. 'And would ye for pity's sake take a look at what's along with him. That ould cod Clancy. And him preenin' himself like a newly-trod laverock. Oh, I knew well he'd be stuck in this business somewhere.'

Clancy, tall, straight-backed, thin as a lath, looked youthful beside the stooped figure of the priest. Never before had I seen anyone so old, so incredibly old and shrunken and withered up.

36

He must have been a big man in his day, but the years had done their work and all that was now left was the massive head sunk, as if by its own weight, into the tired drooping shoulders. You got the impression that this huge encumbrance of a head might at any moment plunge down through the crumbling framework of bone and sagging flesh that had once been a plump clerical body on to the tottering legs beneath. The flesh on the face sagged too and formed a vast dewlap that made the head seem even bigger than it was. Leaning heavily on Clancy's arm, he shuffled along with quick dragging steps the while he champed and mumbled continuously at his toothless gums. Older than time itself he looked. Even his clothes, wrinkled and faded and hanging around him in slack listless folds, seemed like himself to have long since given up the struggle against the intolerable burden of the years.

All the more startling it was when you noticed his eyes – bright and unblinking and ageless as a bird's. They were utterly incongruous – like an owl with the eyes of a canary – but in some queer way they made your heart grow big in your body. I often try to recapture the expression in them. Candour there certainly was. And a childish trust. And tolerance. But there was something else – something fierce and unbeatable and strangely heroic that I'd be the better for remembering.

The two men halted at high-water mark. Around them in a half-circle the crowd ranged itself, silent, watchful, curious.

Clancy faced about. 'Get down on yer knees, all of ye,' he commanded in a loud domineering voice. Everyone obeyed.

He now produced from under his coat a beautifully-fashioned laurel wreath and from an inside pocket, a candle. Fixing the candle upright in the close-plaited stems he handed the wreath to the priest, his manner a mixture of acolyte and ring-master. With a final flourish he struck a match and, shielding the flame in his cupped hands, lit the candle.

In the bright sunlight the flame was invisible and Father Brady remained for a long time gazing in bewilderment at the candle as if wondering if it were really lit. At last he roused himself. Carrying the laurel wreath stiffly at arm's length he shuffled down the shelving beach into the fringe of the receding tide. Tiny wavelets lapped and hissed over the shingle and over his old worn boots but he paid no heed. Carefully, almost tenderly, he placed the wreath on the surface of the water. Then he stepped back and waited.

Almost at once the wreath commenced to drift out on the ebb-tide. It skipped and curtseyed and bobbed up and down on the water, twirling round and round in either direction, stopping and starting in convulsive jerks as though it were dancing a highly indecorous Roger de Coverley. The glossy leaves shone with a wicked sleekness. The little candle flaunted its slim satin-white nakedness before the sun and sea. Gay, impudent, very lovely it was, but without motive or meaning – a bunch of twigs at the mercy of wind and tide; a wretched little pishogue; a tired old man's dream.

As it drifted on and on out to sea I could sense this feeling in the restless crowd. I could see it in Mick Donnelly's sardonic grin. But Father Brady, still standing motionless at the water's edge, had about him an air of certainty, of dogged unswerving certainty.

A sudden stir of excitement drew my attention back to the wreath. It had stopped about twenty fathoms from the shore and was bobbing up and down excitedly, struggling frantically, I thought, to free itself from some obstruction – seaweed or the like. Eventually it seemed to get clear for it drifted off again.

But now its behaviour became entirely abnormal. It commenced to range around in every direction, methodically quartering the surface of the sea, backwards and forwards, this way and that like a hound casting about in a covert. It seemed to quiver with excitement.

Behind me I heard Mick mutter something about whirlpools, but whirlpools or freakish eddies would hardly account for what happened next. As though it had at last picked up the scent the wreath started off across the bay heading for Seal Island, a tall gaunt rock only a stone's throw from the cliffs. This meant that not only was it holding its own against the pull of the swiftly-running ebb-tide but, crazier still, it was sailing right into the eye of a breeze that had just now blown up from the west. Slowly, doggedly, it pushed its way through the water, never once deviating from its self-chosen course. It seemed to have acquired a will and purpose of its own that drove it forward against wind and tide. The more you looked at it the more you became certain that it was a live thing, a thing relentless, single-minded, terrifyingly unselfish like an ant or bee or mayfly – the incarnation of a single overwhelming desire that could only end in fulfilment.

The wreath continued on across the bay into the shadow of Seal Island. There it appeared to hesitate. For perhaps a minute it circled round uncertainly. Then it stopped, lying inertly on the water as though resting on solid ground. Freed from the blurring dazzle of the sun it stood out clear and distinct against the dark background of the rock glowing with a rich warm secret glow – a milk-white opal set in a cameo of jade.

You could not imagine the queer hush that came over all of us. At dusk, when the gulls are straggling home, grey-dim and quiet and ghostly, gliding out and in along the curves of the cliffs, you get the same kind of hush. It is universal. Every sound is muffled and apologetic, an instinctive cringing away from the onslaught of darkness. This was different. Around us the ordinary everyday noises went on as usual – the waves fussing over the shingle, the rumble of a cart on the road above us, a dog barking monotonously, distant voices – but we were cut off in a small world of silence, a world narrowed down to a motionless green and white speck, a strip of glittering wind-wrinkled sea and the sombre druid-like figure of the old priest.

Clancy's arrogant voice broke the spell. He had got to his feet and was shouting orders, instructions, warnings. No one paid the slightest attention to him. The kneeling crowd broke up, scattering in all directions, some towards Seal Island for a better view of the wreath, others making for the quay where already the first boat was nosing out of the harbour entrance. Only Father Brady remained, lonely and unheeded, waiting patiently at the foot of the beach.

It is turning dusk. The lamps in the harbour have just been lit. Inside the boat-house all that the hungry sea has left of the skipper's body is laid out on planks stretched across a couple of trestles, where it will stay till after tomorrow's inquest. Up on the cliff a group of fishermen loll on the grass, their backs against a ditch, listening tolerantly to Mick Donnelly laying down the law.

'I don't know what kind of men ye are at all,' he was saying. 'Ye'd swallow back, so ye would, any kind of an ould fairy-tale that would come yer way. Sure ye know fine well the whole business was a bit of play-actin'. Mebbe ye'll tell me I'm a liar when I remind ye that there's always a sweep of water running across the bay to Seal Island on an ebb-tide. Wasn't that how the Doctor's son was drowned a few years back?'

Someone interrupted: 'Aye, Mick, but it's only after a storm ye'll get the run.'

He is crushed at once. 'Why don't ye go down to the dock and try for yourself? Throw in a bit of a cork and see where it'll land.'

There is an uneasy silence.

Another voice asks: 'What about the wind? Wasn't it blowin' dead against it? And wasn't the candle lightnin' when they picked it up?'

'Wind!' There is a world of scorn in Mick's voice. 'Wind be damned. Sure the sea was as smooth as a baby's bottom.'

He squirts out a jet of tobacco juice with an air of finality, leans his head back on the ditch and pretends to doze off.

No one speaks for a long time. The only sound is the contented gurgling of spittle-choked pipes.

At last Corney Gallagher speaks up: 'Ye're disrememberin' one thing, Mick,' he says in a dreamy offhand kind of way as though talking to himself. Mick just gives a grunt. Corney rambles on as cool as you like: 'Ye know we found the poor ould captain, God rest him, wedged tight under a rock. And I'm thinkin' only for the priest and his bit of greenery he'd be lyin' there still. Aye, and would be till the Day of Judgment.'

Mick sits up furious, nearly choking with rage. 'Ach!' he splutters. 'I don't give a button or a hen's tongue, and that's a damned small piece of meat, whether or which. It was all a pishogue. And a bloody poor one at that.'

Patrick Boyle

Thinking about the story

1 When you read the story, what impression did you get of the place, the kind of people who lived there, and their way of life?
2 Who are the main characters and what are they like?
3 What do you think a pishogue is?
4 What is the meaning of the last paragraph? Why does the story end in this way?

Looking at it in more detail

On your own

Now read through the story again. Search for information about each of these topics and make notes about what you find out.

1 Landscape and the weather
2 Daily life and work
3 Characters: the storyteller, Mick, Clancy, Father Brady
4 Superstition and belief

Groups of 3 or 4

As a group you are going to prepare a presentation about this story for the rest of the class.

1 Discuss each of the topics in turn: tell each other what you have found out.
2 Divide the topics out so that each member of the group has a different topic to work on.
3 Decide how you are going to present your ideas to the class: by talking to them, by means of a poster or wall-chart, as a booklet, or how?
4 Work individually on your chosen topic, so that you use not just your own ideas but those that were contributed by the other members of the group.
5 Bring each person's material together to prepare your final presentation.

Blackbird

Personality and background

We can get a good idea of the storyteller as a person from reading the story. We can also get some idea of her home and everyday life. Read the story again and try to work out as much as you can about her. Write your ideas down, either as continuous writing, or in a table like this:

My idea about her	Quotation/Reason why I think so
Squeamish	'And I hate things like that. I can't bear to touch it.'

Writing anecdotes

This kind of story about something that has happened to you is sometimes called an anecdote. Think of something odd or off-beat that has happened to you or someone you know. (Or, if you can't remember one, make one up.) You are going to tell it to a friend you know well, but instead of telling it in speech, you are going to write it down. As you write, try to catch the tone of voice and the rhythm of speech. (If you are not sure how this is done, look again at the way Carole Senior does it.)

The galloping cat

Reading aloud

The best way to enjoy this poem is to read it aloud.
1 For your first reading, you should ignore the lines the poem is divided into and just follow the sentence punctuation: read it as if it was an ordinary story.
2 Now look at the way it is divided into lines. There is a good reason for the interesting and unusual way this is done. You can begin to explore this by looking at the short lines. Try reading sections that have a short line in them, and leaving a slight pause at the end of the short lines. For example:

> I said:
> Get off! (Be-   [*pause*]
> cause   [*pause*]
> [*now faster*]   I am a cat that likes to
> Gallop about doing good)

3 Now read through the whole poem trying to get the speed and rhythm of the lines right.

What kind of cat?

What impression have you gained of the cat's character from reading the poem? In particular think about these points:
1 What the cat understands by 'doing good'.
2 What it thought the angel was at first and how it reacted.
3 How it reacted when it realized the stranger was an angel.
4 The way it speaks to us.

"I felt a bit sorry for him after I shot his elephant."

The law still allows people to squirt weedkiller in a baby's eyes, inject it with poison, grow cancers on its back, burn its skin off, expose it to radiation and eventually kill it, in unreliable experiments.

So long as it's only an animal.

But you can help stop it.

You don't have to buy products tested on animals.

Please send me ......copies of the Cruelty-Free Products Guide @ 75p each (inc. P&P). I enclose £........
I would like more information on your work ☐
I enclose a donation ☐

NAME
ADDRESS

Send to: The National Anti-Vivisection Society, 51 Harley Street, London W1N 1DD.

This chapter looks at the way in which human beings treat animals. We have immense power over nature – do we use it responsibly? What would animals say about us if they could speak? What would they do to us if they had the chance?

There are suggestions for talking and writing after each item, and further activities on page 67.

"It should be a fantastic parrot. It cost an arm and a leg."

"…And stay out!"

BEWARE OF THE DOG!

"I bet she didn't know her umbrella handle was made of ivory"

Elephant (African)
ENDANGERED SPECIES

The visuals on these two pages were chosen to illustrate different aspects of the relationship between animals and people.

1 What is the point being made in each one?
2 Which do you find most striking and why?
3 Do you think any of them is in bad taste? If so, what are your reasons?
4 If you had to add two or three images to this collage, what would you choose and why?

The newcomer

'There's something new in the river,'
The fish said as it swam –
'It's got no scales, no fins and no gills,
And ignores the impassable dam.'

'There's something new in the trees,'
I heard a bloated thrush sing,
'It's got no beak, no claws, and no feathers,
And not even the ghost of a wing.'

'There's something new in the warren,'
Said the rabbit to the doe.
'It's got no fur, no eyes and no paws,
Yet digs deeper than we dare go.'

'There's something new in the whiteness,'
Said the snow-bright polar bear.
'I saw its shadow on a glacier,
But it left no pawmarks there.'

Through the animal kingdom
The news was spreading fast –
No beak, no claws, no feather,
No scales, no fur, no gills,
It lives in the trees and the water,
In the soil and the snow and the hills,
And it kills and it kills and it kills.

Brian Patten

1 Why is the poem called *The newcomer*?
2 Can you think of an alternative title that sums
   up what it is about?
3 Is it possible to imagine a world in which
   humanity does not 'kill and kill and kill'?
   What would it be like?
4 Is this poem fair to human beings?

Barn owl

Daybreak: the household slept.
I rose, blessed by the sun.
A horny fiend, I crept
out with my father's gun.
Let him dream of a child
obedient, angel-mild –

old No-Sayer, robbed of power
by sleep. I knew my prize
who swooped home at this hour
with daylight-riddled eyes
to his place on a high beam
in our old stables, to dream

light's useless time away.
I stood, holding my breath,
in urine-scented hay,
master of life and death,
a wisp-haired judge whose law
would punish beak and claw.

My first shot struck. He swayed,
ruined, beating his only
wing, as I watched, afraid
by the fallen gun, a lonely
child who believed death clean
and final, not this obscene

bundle of stuff that dropped,
and dribbled through loose straw
tangling in bowels, and hopped
blindly closer. I saw
those eyes that did not see
mirror my cruelty

while the wrecked thing that could
not bear the light nor hide
hobbled in its own blood.
My father reached my side,
gave me the fallen gun.
'End what you have begun.'

I fired. The blank eyes shone
once into mine, and slept.
I leaned my head upon
my father's arm, and wept,
owl-blind in early sun
for what I had begun.

Gwen Harwood

This poem tells the story from the child's point of view. How do you think the father thought and felt about it? Imagine how the story looked from his point of view: how he found out what had happened; what he felt; what he decided to do; what his feelings were about it afterwards. Decide who he is speaking to: his wife? A friend? Another member of the family? Then tell the story from his point of view.

So long, and thanks for all the fish!

Man says he is more intelligent than the dolphin. Well, look: man invented cities, telephones and the ostrich-skin Filofax, did he not?

Dolphins probably think they are more intelligent, because they *don't* live in cities, *don't* speak on the telephone and have *no need* of Filofaxes. That's Douglas Adams' theory (he wrote *Hitchhiker's Guide to the Galaxy*).

Intelligent or not, dolphins have often saved human lives.

Earlier this year, a boy on a surfboard was attacked off Bondi Beach in Australia. A Jaws-sized bite was taken out of the board, and then the shark came in for the kill. The boy was saved by a school of dolphins who came barrelling in and used their hard beaks to beat off the shark.

There is said to be a regular dolphin patrol off the Pacific island of Vanuatu. Small children swim on the beach, safe in the knowledge that no shark will bother them.

In 1945, a Florida woman was saved from drowning by a dolphin. She went swimming on a beach where there was a strong undertow, and was immediately dragged under.

Just before losing consciousness, she remembers hoping that someone would push her ashore.

'With that, someone gave me a tremendous shove, and I landed on the beach, face down, too exhausted to turn over. . . when I did, no one was near, but in the water almost 18 feet out, a dolphin was leaping around.'

Dolphins can be used for the treatment of clinical depression. Patients can be lowered in to the water to play with the dolphins.

'It's magic! Pure magic!' said one. 'You can't get that sort of medicine out of a bottle.'

Some psychiatrists believe that just watching a dolphin on video can have a beneficial effect.

Dolphins are extraordinarily intelligent. Two Swedish scientists report this story. 'Two dolphins enjoyed playing with an eel in their tank. One of the dolphins would catch the eel delicately between its teeth, carry it around for a while, then let it go.

'The other dolphin would catch the eel and swim around, chased by her friend. Then they reversed roles.

'One day the eel managed to hide in a pipe at the bottom of the tank. The dolphin found a poisonous fish that also lived in the tank.

'He carefully caught the fish in his teeth so that it couldn't hurt him, and poked the fish into the pipe where the eel was hiding. The eel zoomed out and the dolphins continued their game of catch.'

No wonder that dolphins have been at the centre of myths and legends for ever. In some parts of the world they are believed to have magical qualities.

According to Jim Nollman, there is a tribe of Aborigines known as the Dolphin People. They live off the north coast of Australia.

For thousands of years, this tribe has been reported to be in communication with the wild Bottlenose dolphins, who live off the coast.

Their Shamans (holy men) remain heirs to a complex series of whistles that signal the dolphins to venture close to shore. The Shamans explain, at that point, they begin to speak to the dolphins mind to mind.

The dolphin is a very special creature. But they are still slaughtered by humans.

And that is a terrible thing to happen.

I don't want to join the navy

Dolphins have been taught to track and kill enemy divers – even though they are among the world's most playful creatures.

The US Navy has more than 100 marine mammals (dolphins, porpoises, seals and whales) in training at ocean bases at any one time. The activities in which the animals are involved are a closely-guarded secret.

'The operational employment of dolphins is classified,' the Pentagon's Lieutenant James Wood told *The Indy*.

Only one operation, termed Quickfind, is not top secret. It uses dolphins and seals to recover military equipment, usually test devices, from the sea bed or the bottom of a lake. The animals are trained to locate and attach a retrieving line to the objects.

The Pentagon, however, prefers not to discuss the use of dolphins as underwater sentries, guarding against, and possibly killing, enemy saboteurs and spies at its Trident nuclear submarine bases in Georgia, Connecticut and Washington.

Though not naturally aggressive, dolphins are powerful creatures. They sometimes use their beaks to ram sharks in the guts, and sometimes kill them.

In 1987, at the height of the tanker-war phase of the Iran-Iraq war, the American government publicly announced that it was sending five dolphins to join its fleet in the Persian Gulf. The animals were to 'provide an underwater surveillance and detection capability.'

At the time, unnamed Defence Department sources said the dolphins would be used to hunt for Iranian mines and guard against attacks by enemy frogmen.

This was not the first time dolphins had been used in battle.

During the Vietnam war in the 1960s they had been sent out as mine-hunters, and to detect underwater attackers at the huge naval base at Cam Rahn Bay.

The American use of dolphins dates back to 1960. That year, the Navy captured and studied a Pacific white-sided dolphin to see if it had qualities which could be applied to the design of torpedoes.

Since 1963 it has used dolphins and other animals for research and practical work as part of the Navy Marine Mammal Program.

The Navy has found that dolphins can be used more safely, efficiently and cost-effectively than human divers (they're cheaper to run).

In the research field, the Navy is keen to develop a system based on the dolphin's in-built echo-location communication system (like sonar).

American officials deny claims that Navy dolphins are maltreated.

One former animal trainer, who worked for the Navy between 1985 and 1988, claimed that dolphins and seals had been kicked, beaten and underfed; 13 of the Navy's dolphins have died in the last three years, over half of them from starvation or stomach disorders.

The Navy replies by saying that the death-rate amongst its dolphins was 'the lowest among all those organizations maintaining significant numbers of marine animals.'

Whatever the truth, the US Navy has not always been a friend to cetaceans (the scientific name for whales and dolphins).

In the summer of 1955, the American air force dropped depth charges on several thousand killer whales off the coast of Iceland after they were accused of destroying fishermen's nets. The whales, it was said, were threatening to halve the annual catch.

Ted Crail, a man interested for many years in whales and dolphins, writes: 'A film exists, made by the Navy, which shows whales dressed in space-age headgear nosing down into the ocean and finding a lost torpedo. The whales clamped a lifting device on to the torpedo with their special headgear, and swam confidently away. A parachute blooms from the device they have installed. The parachute lifts the torpedo to the surface.

'In San Diego, I had spoken with Navy men familiar with the making of the film, and they had told me that not only were the whales marvellous at understanding the process the humans had taught them, but the whales soon felt they understood what was wanted better than clumsy sailors did.

'When the sailors fouled up, the whales would get sore and fuss – in a way that humans could understand.'

When you hear stories like this, you do wonder whether we arc vastly under-rating these vast creatures.

Sean O'Neill,
The Indy

Getting the picture

1 Read both articles to get a general idea of what they are about.
2 Now read them again and make a diagram to show the pattern of the ideas and information they contain. It could be a web diagram:

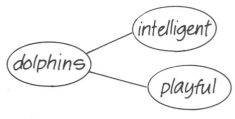

or a series of lists:

Intelligence | Military uses
playing with the eel | searching for mines

or some other method of your own.

Reflecting

Now look at your notes and think about what you have read. Decide what you think is the one most important feature of the material on these two pages. Focus on this. Read those sections again and be prepared to talk about them.

Pair discussion

Discuss your ideas with a partner.

*T*en green bottles

Characters

The characters could be male or female, depending on the people playing them. The names in the text should be altered accordingly.

    Doris/Dennis the Dog
    Katie/Kevin the Cat
    Rachel/Raymond the Rabbit
    Maisie/Michael the Mouse
    Min/Jim the Chimp
    Hat/Pat the Rat

An animal experiment laboratory. The animals are in their respective cages. It is morning and the animals are slowly waking up.

Pat: *(Sings to the tune of 'Ten Green Bottles')* One green bottle, standing in a row, one green bottle standing in a row. . .

Dennis: Knock it off, Pat, you know you can't sing. . .

Ray: That's right. Shut up or they'll be round to slit your vocal cords!

Dennis: Hey! Heard about the frog who had his vocal cords cut?

Ray: No. What happened to him?

Dennis: He croaked!

Ray: *(Puzzled)* How could he croak when they'd cut his. . .*(Getting the joke)* Oh, croaked!. . .*(He chuckles)* Nice one Dennis! Croaked! What a joker!

Pat: *(Sings)* Two green bottles standing in a row. . .

Ray: Shut up!

    Katie the Cat *wakes up.*

Ray: *(To* **Katie***)* Morning!

Katie: Morning.

Ray: Another wonderful day. It's good to be alive!

Katie: Is it?

Dennis: Oh, don't start moaning again. Honestly, you really are a miserable specimen.

Katie: Exactly right! We're all miserable specimens.

    Dennis *is about to reply but is stopped by two white-coated handlers, bringing in a mouse. The mouse is squeaking with fright. They put the mouse in the cage next to Raymond's, then leave.*

Ray: And who do we have here?

Maisie: *(Frightened)* M. . .M. . .M. . .Maisie.

Dennis: *(Jokingly)* M. . .M. . .M. . .Maisie? Are you in here to aid research into stammering?

    Ray *and* **Dennis** *burst into laughter.*

Katie: Dennis! Can't you see she's frightened?

Dennis: Sorry, only joking. *(To* **Maisie***)* Only joking.

Katie: *(Kindly)* Are you all right?

Maisie: *(Beginning to calm down)* I'm scared.

Katie: What's your name?

Maisie: Maisie the Mouse.

Dennis: Maisie, hey? Well Maisie, welcome to the lab. The place where we privileged animals help the human race push forward the frontiers of scientific knowledge. Allow me to introduce you to the honoured guests of the establishment. I'm Dennis the Dog, and that's Katie the Cat . . .

Katie: Hello, Maisie.

Dennis: . . .And that's good old Raymond Rabbit twitching his nose.

Ray: That's me, Maisie. Laugh a minute Ray, the sunshine of the day. *(He points at* **Jim the Chimp***)* And over there is Jim the Chimp. Morning, Jim.

    Jim *coughs in reply.*

Ray: Still coughing then, Jim? How many are you on now? (**Jim** *holds up ten fingers, three times)* Thirty a day, eh? Cutting down then.

Maisie: What does he do?

Katie: Smokes cigarettes.

Maisie: Why?

Dennis: Because humans need to know how dangerous cigarettes are. Jim used to be on fifty a day, but the price has gone up and the lab has had to make financial cutbacks, so he's not smoking so many now.

50

Katie: It's disgusting!

Dennis: That's what I said. How on earth can you do proper research without proper financial backing? Cutbacks are a terrible thing. Some experiments have had to be scrapped!

Katie: I meant forcing Jim to smoke is disgusting.

Maisie: But humans know cigarettes are dangerous, don't they?

Katie: Of course.

Maisie: Why do they make them then?

Dennis: Ah, well. . .

Katie: They could stop if they wanted to, and then Jim wouldn't have to smoke any more, and he wouldn't cough like that.

They are interrupted by **Pat the Rat**.

Pat: *(Singing)* Three green bottles standing in a row. . .

Maisie: *(Frightened)* Oh, who's that?

Dennis: It's only Pat the Rat. . .

Ray: Not again, Pat. Will you shut up!

Maisie: What's the matter with him?

Dennis: Oh, very sad case. He went mad in the mazes.

Ray: Yeah, they put him in these mazes, see, and every time he found his way to a white door, he got a piece of food and every time he found his way to a black door, he got an electric shock.

Maisie: Oh, how awful.

Katie: That wasn't what drove him mad, though: nothing so simple. They started switching things about, putting the food behind the black

51

door and the shock behind the white door. After that they put shocks behind both doors for a bit. Then they changed the colours of the doors to blue and red. . .

Dennis: Drove him bonkers in the end. He doesn't say anything now, just sings that song all day.

Maisie: That's horrible!

Ray: It is pretty bad, but it's better than 'One man went to mow. . .'

Maisie: Not the song, what they did to him! Will they do that to me?
(She begins to cry)

Katie: Of course not. *(She stares pointedly at **Ray** and **Dennis**)*

Ray: *(Uneasily)* Oh, er, no, of course they won't. Will they, Den?

Dennis: No, no. Don't worry, Maisie, we have great fun here, don't we Ray?

Ray: Oh yes. Some great laughs. Remember George the Gerbil?

Dennis: George?

Ray: The one they did the brain transplant on.

Dennis: *(Remembering)* Oh yes, that George.

Ray: See, Maisie, they gave him the brain of a budgie.

Maisie: *(Still sniffling)* Why?

Ray: I think they wanted to see if a gerbil could learn to fly.

Maisie: And did he?

Ray: Fly? He couldn't even sit on his perch without falling off – and you should have heard him trying to say, 'Who's a pretty boy, then?'

Dennis: That was a laugh.

Ray: Mind you, not half as funny as the budgie looked trying to wash its whiskers with its wings!

Ray and **Dennis** *roar with laughter.* **Maisie** *cries.* **Katie** *looks disgusted.*

Katie: Shut up! It's wicked. How dare they?

Dennis: *(Patiently)* Look, Katie. Humans are a higher type of being. It's the natural order.

Katie: If they're a higher type of being, they should know how to behave.

Pat: *(Sings)* Four green bottles standing in a row, four green bottles standing in a row. . .

Ray: For goodness sake, Pat. Put a sock in it. Your singing's awful and you've got the words all wrong, anyway. . .

Dennis: Hey, remember old Sammy Sheep? This'll kill you, Maisie. We had a real laugh with him. It was a giggle, wasn't it, Ray?

Maisie: What happened?

Dennis: They gave him two heads!

Ray: That's right! And his left hand head always wanted to go one way and his right hand head wanted to go the other way, and he kept falling over. You had to laugh, didn't you?

Dennis: Oh, we roared! Funniest thing I've ever seen!

Katie: *(Viciously)* Not very funny for him, was it?

There is an uncomfortable pause. **Jim** *coughs in the background.*

Dennis: Well, I s'pose not, not for him. Not funny for him.

Pat: *(Sings)* Five green bottles standing in a row. . .

Ray: I won't tell you again. Shut up!

Katie: And look what they're doing to Gary the Guinea Pig.

Dennis: That research is necessary!

Katie: *(Angry)* Necessary! Squeezing toothpaste into his eyes! Where's the sense in that? You don't put toothpaste in your eyes, do you? You put it on your teeth.

Dennis: Well, you might look into the nozzle to see if there's any left, and then squeeze the tube too hard. Anyway, he shouldn't make so much noise about it. All that screaming, it's enough to put me off my food additives.

Pat: *(Sings)* Six green bottles standing in a row, six green bottles standing in a row. . .

Ray: Pat, you're driving us crazy! Be quiet!

Katie: And what happened to the hamsters we had in here last week? I'll tell you what happened. They were given some new medicine to try out, something to do with reducing weight. They all turned green, their fur fell out and they all curled up like crisp packets in a fire and started speaking Swedish.

Ray: Cor, I wish I'd seen that – what a giggle!

Katie: *(Looking at* **Ray** *with immense distaste)* Then they all died. But d'you want to know the really funny part? The lab down the road did the same experiment last year, with the same result, but they kept quiet about it. So all those hamsters died for nothing.

Pat: *(Sings)* Seven green bottles standing in a row, seven green bottles standing in a row. . .

Ray: I swear, I'm going to kill him!

Dennis: *(Defensively)* Well, they were only hamsters. Rodents are a fairly low form of life. . .

Maisie: Oh! *(She cries)*

Dennis: *(Hastily)* . . . Present company excepted, of course.

Katie: Low form of life, eh? And what are you then, Dogbreath?

Dennis: *(With dignity)* We dogs are much closer in nature to humans.

Katie: Then you should be ashamed.

Again there is an uncomfortable pause. **Jim** *continues to cough in the background.*

Ray: *(Attempting to lighten the mood)* Hey, Katie, how's that new hairspray you're trying?

Katie: *(Sarcastically)* Oh, wonderful.

Ray: Does it control your hair naturally, while giving it a silky shine and a brilliant glow?

Katie: How should I know? They don't put it on my hair, they squirt it up my nose.

Dennis: You should try it, Raymond.

Ray: Why?

Dennis: 'Cos it's a hare-spray. Get it? Hare-spray!

Ray: *(Not amused for once)* I'm not a hare, I'm a rabbit.

Dennis: Well, same thing, isn't it?

Ray: No, it isn't. How would you like it if I said you were a hyena?

Dennis: Watch it!

Pat: Eight green bottles standing in a row. . .

Ray *and* **Dennis** *turn their anger on* **Pat**.

Ray: I warned you, Pat!

Dennis: Yeah, he warned you!

Maisie: Oh, please don't start a fight. I can't bear it – everything's so dreadful here without us animals fighting as well. I'm so frightened.

Dennis: *(Calming down)* There, there, don't worry, you'll be all right.

Katie: What do you mean, 'all right'? We're none of us going to be all right.

    Maisie *sobs.*

Dennis: That's very tactful, Katie. Cheer her up, why don't you? Look Maisie, they'll probably do one teensy little experiment on you that won't hurt a bit. . .

Pat: *(Sings)* Nine green bottles standing in a row, nine green bottles standing in a row. . .

Dennis: Pat! As I was saying, they'll do a little experiment on you, that won't hurt a bit, and then they'll let you go.

Katie: Who are you trying to fool? There's only one way out of here, when they've finished with you – through the incinerator.

    Maisie *goes into hysterics.*

Ray: Now look what you've done. There, there.

Dennis: I don't like that sort of talk.

Katie: Go on then, what have I said that isn't true?

Dennis: I, er. . .*(Tries to think of something. He gives up)* I never said it wasn't true. Look, humans have to do their experiments.

Katie: Why? Why do they have to squirt hairspray up my nose?

Dennis: To see if it's safe if they sniff it accidentally.

Katie: If they're stupid enough to sniff hairspray, they deserve to get ill. Filthy stuff.

Dennis: That's not the point. . .

Katie: What do they want hairsprays for, anyway? Have you ever seen an animal using one? If they're so keen on hairsprays, why don't they squirt them up each others' noses?

Dennis: Now you're just being unreasonable.

Katie: Unreasonable??!!

Dennis: Human beings are cleverer than we are. They say they need these experiments, and they know best.

Katie: Who says they know best?

Dennis: They do.

Katie: Aha!

Dennis: Well it's obvious isn't it? They're cleverer and stronger and they've got tanks and televisions and beefburgers and pot noodles and yo-yos and all that.

Katie: But why does that give them the right to starve us and choke us and drown us and cut bits off us and stick bits on us and hurt us and kill us? Why do they do it?

Jim: *(Unexpectedly)* They do it. . .*(Cough, cough). . .*because they can.

    Jim *goes into a coughing spasm. There is an uncomfortable silence. Nobody looks at anybody else. Two handlers enter. They are wearing white coats and dark glasses. They seize* **Raymond**.

Dennis: Oh, you off then, Ray?

Ray: Looks like it. Wonder what it is today? Well, see you later. Be good. Cheer up, Maisie, it may never happen.

Ray *is dragged out.*

Katie: 'Bye. Good luck, Ray.

Dennis: Cheers, Ray. Cor, what a character. Good old Ray.

From offstage, there is a horrible tortured scream from **Ray**. *It is suddenly cut off. Even* **Maisie** *stops sobbing, too horrified to cry. Pause.*

Dennis: Oh, ah. D'you reckon we should save Ray some breakfast?

Katie: Not much point is there?

Pat: *(Sings)* Ten green bottles standing in a row,
Ten small specimens, floating to and fro,
But if Humans thought,
One day that's where they'd go. . .
There'd be no more bottles standing in a row.

Steve Barlow and *Steve Skidmore*

---

1 Did you laugh when you read this play?
2 If so, which parts of it made you laugh?
3 Would you describe it as a 'funny' play?
4 If so, what kind of humour does it contain?
5 Do you think this play is for, or against, experiments on animals? What are your reasons for saying so?
6 Who do you think was the cleverest animal in the play, and why?
7 Why do you think the play is called *Ten green bottles*?
8 At what points in the play does Hat/Pat sing his/her song?
9 Why is one bottle *added* each time? Can you see a pattern?

Barney

August 30th

We are alone on the island now, Barney and I. It was something of a jolt to have to sack Tayloe after all these years, but I had no alternative. The petty vandalisms I could have forgiven, but when he tried to poison Barney out of simple malice, he was standing in the way of scientific progress. That I cannot condone.

I can only believe the attempt was made while under the influence of alcohol, it was so clumsy. The poison container was overturned and a trail of powder led to Barney's dish. Tayloe's defence was of the flimsiest. He denied it. Who else then?

September 2nd

I am taking a calmer view of the Tayloe affair. The monastic life here must have become too much for him. That, and the abandonment of his precious guinea pigs. He insisted to the last that they were better suited than Barney to my experiments. They were more his speed, I'm afraid. He was an earnest and willing worker, but something of a clod, poor fellow.

At last I have complete freedom to carry on my work without the mute reproaches of Tayloe. I can only ascribe his violent antagonism towards Barney to jealousy. And now that he has gone, how much happier Barney appears to be! I have given him complete run of the place, and what sport it is to observe how his newly awakened intellectual curiosity carries him about. After only two weeks of glutamic acid treatments, he has become interested in my library, dragging the books from the shelves, and going over them page by page. I am certain he knows there is some knowledge to be gained from them had he but the key.

September 8th

For the past two days I have had to keep Barney confined and how he hates it. I am afraid that when my experiments are completed I shall have to do away with Barney. Ridiculous as it may sound there is still the possibility that he might be able to communicate his intelligence to others of his kind. However small the chance may be, the risk is too great to ignore. Fortunately there is, in the basement, a vault built with the idea of keeping vermin out and it will serve equally well to keep Barney in.

September 9th

Apparently I have spoken too soon. This morning I let him out to frisk around a bit before commencing a new series of tests. After a quick survey of the room he returned to his cage, sprang up on the door handle, removed the key with his teeth, and before I could stop him, he was out the window. By the time I reached the yard I spied him on the coping of the well, and I arrived on the spot only in time to hear the key splash into the water below.

I own I am somewhat embarrassed. It is the only key. The door is locked. Some valuable papers are in separate compartments inside the vault.

Fortunately, although the well is over forty feet deep, there are only a few feet of water in the bottom, so the retrieving of the key does not present an insurmountable obstacle. But I must admit Barney has won the first round.

September 10th

I have had a rather shaking experience, and once more in a minor clash with Barney I have come off second best. In this instance I will admit he played the hero's role and may even have saved my life.

In order to facilitate my descent into the well I knotted a length of three-quarter-inch rope at one-foot intervals to make a rude ladder. I reached the bottom easily enough, but after only a few minutes of groping for the key, my flashlight gave out and I returned to the surface. A few feet from the top I heard excited squeaks from Barney, and upon obtaining ground level I observed that the rope was almost completely severed. Apparently it had chafed against the edge of the masonry and the little fellow perceiving my plight had been doing his utmost to warn me.

I have now replaced that section of rope and arranged some old sacking beneath it to prevent a recurrence of the accident. I have replenished the batteries in my flashlight and am now prepared for the final descent. These few moments I have taken off to give myself a breathing spell and to bring my journal up to date. Perhaps I should fix myself a sandwich as I may be down there longer than seems likely at the moment.

September 11th

Poor Barney is dead an soon I shell be the same. He was a wonderfull ratt and life without him is knot worth livving. If anybody reeds this please do not disturb anything on the island but leeve it like it is as a shryn to Barney, espechilly the old well. Do not look for my body as I will caste myself into the see. You mite bring a couple of young ratts an leeve them as a living memorial to Barney. Females – no males. I sprayned my wrist is why this is written so bad. This is my laste will. Do what I say an don't come back or disturb anything after you bring the young ratts like I said. Just females. Goodby

Will Stanton

1 The titles of stories like this have to be chosen carefully. They must not give too much of the plot away. This title doesn't give anything away. Think of two different titles for the story:
   ● one that hints at what the story is about but does not tell the reader everything
   ● one that gives a much clearer idea of what the story is about.

2 What does this story tell us of the author's feelings about:
   ● scientists?
   ● animals (especially rats)?
   ● using animals for experiments?

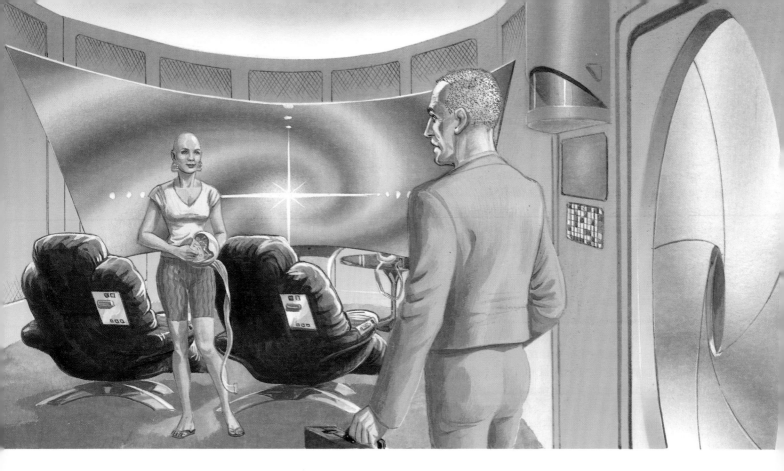

That's show biz!

The iris door opened and before he could even get through to the lounge Loise was talking to him. 'It's the big game show tonight, Hal.'

'And don't I know it,' he replied. 'Everyone is talking about it and the vacuum tubes were packed solid.'

'Everyone wants to get home early to be sure they don't miss it,' Loise said. 'What are you having for dinner?'

He thought about that, then said, 'Make mine a chicken salad with plenty of garlic salt. I'll have pineapple for dessert.'

Loise programmed the computer, pressed out the code for the cookery index and then ordered the meal. 'I'm going to have a curry,' she said. 'Central Kitchens are getting better at making curry.'

Hal pulled out the videoframe reflector so that it almost encapsulated the recliner couch, and Loise waited at the receptor for the food. The salad came out first, making her jump with fright as it landed on the chrome tray; then the curry slid down the chute. Dessert would come later.

'How long before the show?' Hal asked.

'Any minute now,' said Loise, pulling back the foil cover from her dinner. 'This smells delicious, Hal. I don't know why you don't try some.'

'Can't abide food which has been messed about with,' he said, turning up his nose at it.

60

The videoscreen lit up with a thousand dancing lights, crazy dots tumbling over each other, mixing colours, weaving and darting. When the videoframe reflector was warmed through, the colours enclosed them so that they were no longer just watching a videoframe. They were living in it.

There was a fanfare of electronic music, then Robert Henry came on the screen as large as life. It was almost as if he was right there, in the lounge, talking to them. 'Good evening, folks. Welcome to the big game show – and, boy, do we have a show for you tonight!' He smiled so that his audience could see his thousand-dollar teeth transplants.

'I think he's nice,' said Loise. 'He acts natural.'

Hal fished around the salad suspiciously with the polyprilene fork. 'He's a creep.'

'Tonight is the big night,' Robert Henry continued. 'Tonight, live from our security studio, Intervision Projects Limited bring you the big game show. Our sponsors for this evening are that well-known deodorant company, "Nice Bod". Nice Bod spray-on deodorant keeps you fresh and sweet-smelling the whole day through, folks. If you would like to try a free sample, just programme up this number on your computers at home and stand beneath the medical shower. The free body spray comes to you with the compliments of "Nice Bod". Remember the name, folks.'

'I think I'll try some of that,' said Loise.

'Then wait until after the show,' Hal told her. 'I don't want to have to keep pushing the videoframe backwards and forwards all evening.'

'Grumpy patch,' Loise said. 'What's got into you this evening? You should be happy. It's a great night.' She talked to Hal with her eyes stuck to the videoscreen, forking immense quantities of curry into her ever-open mouth. Hal pushed his salad away. 'Where did you put my sensory skin?'

'It's there, on the table,' said Loise. 'I greased the electrodes for you this afternoon. If you had been home earlier there would have been time for you to shave your head.'

'My head doesn't need shaving,' Hal told her. He ran his hand over his head. 'I had a shave for the football match last week.'

'Well, I shaved today,' Loise said. 'I always shave my head smooth when there's a good programme on so that the electrodes stick on properly. They don't make good contact with your head if you leave stubble on.'

He looked over at her and smiled. 'To think that you once had such a fine head of hair. It was like a red river, running down over your shoulders, almost to your waist. The sensory helmet has a lot to answer for, Loise.'

'I'm quite used to it now,' she said, her eyes watching the moving mouth of Robert Henry. 'Shall I turn the sound up so we can both hear what he is saying?'

'Yes,' said Hal. 'Might as well. I think he's through with the commercials now.'

Robert Henry was warming through, his smile getting bigger and bigger all the while. 'And who is our guest artist tonight? You've seen him on your videoframes before, but never, ever, have you seen him in a live big game hunt. Ladies and gentlemen, it is my proud pleasure to introduce to you the greatest big game hunter in the world. Yes, you're right. It's the one and only Buck Evans! Give him a big, big welcome everyone!'

The electronic brass fanfare sounded as Loise clapped her hands in pure excitement, her face illuminated by the colours of the videoscreen. 'Buck Evans!' she cried. 'You hear that, Hal? It's Buck Evans – live!'

'Yes, I hear,' said Hal. 'Where did you put the dessert?'

'Yours didn't arrive,' said Loise. 'Anyway, you can't leave now. Buck Evans is coming on. This is going to be a *live* show, Hal. You can't miss that.'

Robert Henry was talking to the great hunter. 'Tell me, Buck, how does it feel to be doing a live show before an estimated audience of eighty-two million people?'

Buck Evans, unable to blush, simulated nervousness. He sat on the studio chair, a well-tailored leg draped casually over the arm of the chair. 'Well, Robert,' he said, 'I *can* call you Robert?' The announcer beamed, nodding his permission. 'Good,' said Buck Evans. 'I like to call people by their first names. Makes everything all sociable, don't it?'

'He's too calm to be true,' Hal said. 'I bet this is a taped show. He wouldn't be that calm if this was a live transmission.'

While Buck Evans talked to the announcer, Loise and Hal pulled their sensory helmets over their shaven heads, making sure that the greased electrodes were properly in position. They plugged the wires into the recliner arms and pressed the test buttons to see that the helmets were functioning correctly. Then Robert Henry spoke to them again.

'Those of you lucky enough to own sensory helmets should put them on about now. Buck Evans will be wearing a sensory transmitter throughout the big game hunt and you will be able to experience everything Buck is feeling.'

'I still don't know how they do that,' said Loise. 'How can they make you feel what he is feeling?'

Hal gave out a sigh and explained it to her again. 'Trouble is, you never listen to anything,' he said. 'The sensory helmet on Buck Evans's head picks up his brain signals and transmits them to the appropriate areas on your sensory helmet. When he gives off brainwaves in a certain area of his brain, you feel them too and so your brain gets stimulated. It's all done electrically – nothing very wonderful about it.'

'Well, I think it's wonderful,' said Loise. 'I watched a love film yesterday and I swear I fell in love with the leading man. The sensory helmet makes everything so real. No wonder they banned the use of it for advertisements.'

'Now, folks,' Robert Henry said, 'I want your full attention. This is going to be a tough hunt and those people with a yellow code, or a medical fitness rating below 80, ought not to watch. Intervision Projects and Nice Bod deodorants will not hold themselves responsible for any person using a sensory helmet. You wear the helmet at your own risk. We have to issue a warning,' he said, breaking out into his famous smile again. 'We wouldn't want to be responsible for some dear old lady having a heart attack just because her brain got over-stimulated watching our show!' Robert Henry stood under the studio lights, glass dust perspiration bubbling out from his forehead and running in thin rivulets down his face. In the background they could make out the tall figure of Buck Evans pulling on his sensory skin, letting the tailwire transmitter aerial hang down behind. Then he pulled a wig over his helmet so it didn't show.

'You should get a wig,' Hal told Loise. 'Get a red wig and wear it over your sensory skin. I'll get you one for your birthday, if you like.'

'Quiet,' said Loise. 'Buck Evans is going to talk.'

The big game hunter ambled up to the videocamera, adjusting his wig so that the pink sensory skin was out of sight. 'Good evening everyone,' he said. 'It is my financial pleasure to be with you tonight.' That got a big laugh, even though it was an old joke. 'As you know, I will be wearing my sensory skin so that you can feel what I am feeling, and I'll tell you one thing for sure – I won't be feeling happy! Just remember, this is a live show and I have no idea what is going to happen. When that tiger comes at me, I'll be fighting for my life and I have no idea what it's going to do to your sensory helmets. If you get too excited, you just pull the plug on me and watch it on your videoframes instead.'

'He makes such a big deal out of it,' Hal grumbled.

'That's showmanship,' said Loise. 'Anyway, I doubt that you would want to take his place. I certainly wouldn't!'

Suddenly the videoframe darkened and the scene changed. Hal and Loise sat back as the videoscreen built up a jungle scene with trees and green grass and all manner of exotic growing things.

'They do the scenery good,' said Loise. 'I could just watch them making electronic scenery all evening.'

The jungle picture wavered and Buck Evans came in from the left, carrying a long-barrelled rifle. He gave a cheery wave to the studio audience and another to the videocamera. 'OK, I'm ready,' he said.

As Buck Evans walked along the studio floor, the projected image moved too. When he stopped, the picture froze. Hal and Loise could feel the tension inside themselves, knowing that they were feeling Buck Evans's fears and excitements. Then they saw the tiger.

'Look out!' Loise screamed.

'He can't hear you,' said Hal.

But Buck Evans had seen the tiger and his rifle was already at his shoulder. He squeezed the trigger, and missed. The tiger growled and slunk off into the bushes ahead.

'This is exciting,' said Loise. 'I've never known Buck Evans to miss a shot.'

'Probably did it on purpose,' said Hal. 'He did it just to get us excited. But don't worry, he'll get it with the next shot. He has to.'

'I think the studio should give him more than two shots,' said Loise. 'It isn't fair to just allow two.'

'The studio know what they are doing,' Hal told her. 'With a two-shot big game hunt, the audience know they are in for some excitement.'

So they sat back in their recliners, following Buck Evans through the electronic jungle, hearing the leaves swish in the mild breeze, feeling the breeze as Buck Evans was feeling it; sweating at the tension, just as Buck Evans was sweating at it.

'What if he *had* hit the tiger?' Loise asked. 'How do they make the tiger do what he does?'

'The tiger is just a film,' said Hal. 'If the electronic rifle had lined up with the tiger, the film on the computer would have changed and you would have seen the reel where the tiger falls down dead. If his aim had just wounded the tiger, the computer would have selected a reel for the sort of wound inflicted and then played that through the videocamera. It all depends how he lines up the rifle.'

'So the film just carries on as normal if he misses?'

'Yes, unless he does something stupid. If he makes a loud noise, the computer in the studio would pick it up and transmit a different film causing the tiger to attack. What film appears on the videoscreen depends entirely on what Evans does. He makes the films change.'

They were still following Evans through the lush, dense jungle, feeling his heart thump-thumping against his ribs, feeling the sweat collecting on their foreheads just as it was collecting on his.

When the tiger did appear again, Loise let out a wild yell. 'There he is!' She felt Buck Evans's heart lurch and the surge of adrenalin went through her brain as he lifted his rifle. But the tiger was already launched in mid-air, jaws gaping wild. Evans pulled the trigger, sweeping the rifle upwards.

'He missed!' Loise yelled. 'Jumping cats! He missed again!'

Hal leaned forward, turning up the sensory helmet so that he could feel Buck Evans's emotions at full blast. 'I never thought to see such a thing,' he breathed. 'It's incredible! Fancy Buck Evans missing two shots like that.'

The jungle disappeared and the tiger disappeared and the studio lights went on. Hal could see that no one in the audience was prepared for what had happened. A woman was weeping and some people were getting up to leave.

Robert Henry came out before the videocamera, his face long and drawn. 'Well, folks, I never thought it would come to this but, after all, big game hunting is a dangerous pastime. Buck Evans is a great sport and he finally met his match.'

And, as he talked, men were erecting the polyprilene transparent screen around the far end of the studio.

'Come over here and say something to the people,' said Robert Henry.

Buck Evans came over to the camera and gave the ghost of a smile. Loise could feel his heart thump-thump-thumping away through her sensory skin helmet.

'We sure will be sorry to lose you,' said Robert Henry. 'You were the world's greatest big game hunter, Buck. We all admire you for your courage.'

'Thanks, Robert,' Buck Evans replied. 'When a man goes out for a big cat, he has to take the risks. I knew the score and now I have lost.'

Without further words, Buck Evans turned and went through the security door in the polyprilene screen. He raised his hand above his head, then let it drop. It was the signal.

At the far end of the studio a trapdoor opened up and eighty-two million viewers felt the screaming surge of fear as a real live tiger came bounding up from the studio menagerie to face the greatest big game hunter in the world.

And when it was over, Loise removed her hot, sticky sensory helmet and smiled at Hal. 'Pity he had to go,' she said. 'I quite liked him. Anyway, with animals now protected by the government, it's the only way to get excitement out of big game hunting. This way the hunter gets his thrills and the animal has a chance if the hunter misses with a computer shot.'

'That was great,' said Hal. 'That's what I call real entertainment.'

Terry Tapp

World of the future

The story is based on a number of ideas about how society may develop.

Evidence	Comment
ordering dinner	They must have a kind of central kitchen connected to all the houses by chutes so that when you order food it is delivered automatically.
videoframe reflector	

Individual research

Read through it again, looking for evidence of what the author thinks this world of the future will be like. List the evidence you find and comment on what you think it means. You could do it in the form of a table like this:

Group work

1 Discuss your ideas with the rest of your group.
2 Together make a full list of all the information and ideas you have got.
3 Decide how to present your ideas to the rest of the class (eg poster, spoken report).
4 Prepare a presentation for the rest of the class.

Taking it further

What would it be like to live in this future world? Think about its good and its bad points. Then make up a scene between Loise and Hal that illustrates your feelings about it. You can present your ideas:
- as a story
- as a playscript
- as an improvised scene
- on audio- or video-tape.

Barn owl

This poem tells a simple story, but the lessons that the writer draws from it are more complex.

1 In the first verse the storyteller contrasts what she thinks she is like with how she believes her father sees her. What words does she use and why does she choose them?

2 In verse 2, how does she describe her father? What does this phrase mean? Does it help us understand why she wants to shoot the owl?

3 In the third verse she describes herself as 'a wisp-haired judge'. What is the point of this comparison?

4 At the end of the poem she weeps for what she 'had begun'. What had she begun?

5 What lesson do you think the writer wants us to draw from the poem?

Ten green bottles

Thumbnail sketches: individual work

Although this play is about animals, it treats them as if they were people, with clearly defined characters. (This is called anthropomorphism.) Make a list of the characters and against their names, write very brief descriptions of their most important characteristics. For example you might write:

Ray: funny, witty, devil-may-care

Presenting the play: group work

Discuss how you could present this play. How will you tackle the problem of acting as animals on stage? Think about these possibilities:

1 Using movement to represent the qualities of each animal.

2 Using voice to show what each of them is like.

3 Using masks.

4 Doing it as a radio play.

Barney/That's show biz!

Both these stories could be described as science fiction: they look at the way in which human beings have treated animals up to now and then ask the question, 'What would happen if. . .?' By doing this they make us think about the present (what we are doing now) and the future (what we should do from now on). What do you think are the most important things they have to say about both the present and the future?

The chapter as a whole

Think about the things you have read and the illustrations you have looked at in this chapter. Think, too, about the activities you have taken part in.

● Which did you find most interesting?

● Which made you think most?

● Which did you find most difficult?

● Which did you like least?

● Have any of them made you change your opinions about animals and the way we treat them?

When you have considered these points, write down your own commentary on the chapter and the work you did.

Relativity

The things we learn from our relatives!
The things we learn about them!
This chapter shows us a family learning together and what one young boy learned about life from his grandmother. But first: brothers and sisters. Each item is followed by suggestions for talking and writing.

What is this cartoon saying about brothers and sisters? Do you agree with it? Make up a ninth frame which shows us what Lucy is thinking.

Sisters

(for Marian)

My sister
was the bad one –
said what she thought
and did what she liked
and didn't care.

At ten she wore
a knife tucked in
her leather belt,
dreamed of *being*
a prince on a white horse.

Became a dolly bird
with dyed hair longer
than her skirts, pulling
the best of the local talent.
Mother wept and prayed.

At thirty she's divorced,
has cropped her locks
and squats in Hackney –
tells me 'God created man
then realized Her mistake.'

I'm not like her,
I'm good – but now
I'm working on it.
Fighting through
to my own brand of badness

I am glad of her
at last – her conferences,
her anger, and her boots.
We talk and smoke
and laugh at everybody –

two bad sisters.

Wendy Cope

What's in a word?

Two key words in this poem are: *sisters   bad*
1 What does each one normally mean to you?
2 In what special way is each one used in the poem?
3 How does Wendy Cope make use of this combination
   of meanings?

Mother's version

'Mother wept and prayed.'
Think about the mother's thoughts and feelings about
the two sisters:
1 when they were young;
2 now that the teller of the story is 'fighting through
   to her own brand of badness'.
Imagine that she talks to a close friend at these two
different stages in her life, and tells her about her daughters.
Write two short conversations in which she reveals her
thoughts and feelings.

The all-American slurp

The first time our family was invited out to dinner in America, we disgraced ourselves while eating celery. We had emigrated to this country from China, and during our early days here we had a hard time with American table manners.

In China we never ate celery raw, or any other kind of vegetable raw. We always had to disinfect the vegetables in boiling water first. When we were presented with our first relish tray, the raw celery caught us unprepared.

We had been invited to dinner by our neighbors, the Gleasons. After arriving at the house, we shook hands with our hosts and packed ourselves into a sofa. As our family of four sat stiffly in a row, my younger brother and I stole glances at our parents for a clue as to what to do next.

Mrs Gleason offered the relish tray to Mother. The tray looked pretty, with its tiny red radishes, curly sticks of carrots, and long, slender stalks of pale green celery. 'Do try some of the celery, Mrs Lin,' she said. 'It's from a local farmer, and it's sweet.'

Mother picked up one of the green stalks, and Father followed suit. Then I picked up a stalk, and my brother did too. So there we sat, each with a stalk of celery in our right hand.

Mrs Gleason kept smiling. 'Would you like to try some of the dip, Mrs Lin? It's my own recipe: sour cream and onion flakes, with a dash of Tabasco sauce.'

Most Chinese don't care for dairy products, and in those days I wasn't even ready to drink fresh milk. Sour cream sounded perfectly revolting. Our family shook our heads in unison.

Mrs Gleason went off with the relish tray to the other guests, and we carefully watched to see what they did. Everyone seemed to eat the raw vegetables quite happily.

Mother took a bite of her celery. *Crunch.* 'It's not bad!' she whispered.

Father took a bite of his celery. *Crunch.* 'Yes, it *is* good,' he said, looking surprised.

I took a bite, and then my brother. *Crunch, crunch.* It was more than good; it was delicious. Raw celery has a slight sparkle, a zingy taste that you don't get in cooked celery. When Mrs Gleason came around with the relish tray, we each took another stalk of celery, except my brother. He took two.

There was only one problem: long strings ran through the length of the stalk, and they got caught in my teeth. When I help my mother in the kitchen, I always pull the strings out before slicing celery.

I pulled the strings out of my stalk. *Z-z-zip, z-z-zip.* My brother followed suit. *Z-z-zip, z-z-zip, z-z-zip.* To my left, my parents were taking care of their own stalks. *Z-z-zip, z-z-zip, z-z-zip.*

Suddenly I realized that there was dead silence except for our zipping. Looking up, I saw that the eyes of everyone in the room were on our family. Mr and Mrs Gleason, their daughter Meg, who was my friend, and their neighbors the Badels – they were all staring at us as we busily pulled the strings of our celery.

That wasn't the end of it. Mrs Gleason announced that dinner was served and invited us to the dining table. It was lavishly covered with platters of food, but we couldn't see any chairs around the table. So we helpfully carried over some dining chairs and sat down. All the other guests just stood there.

Mrs Gleason bent down and whispered to us, 'This is a buffet dinner. You help yourselves to some food and eat it in the living room.'

Our family beat a retreat back to the sofa as if chased by enemy soldiers. For the rest of the evening, too mortified to go back to the dining table, I nursed a bit of potato salad on my plate.

Next day Meg and I got on the school bus together. I wasn't sure how she would feel about me after the spectacle our family made at the party. But she was just the same as usual, and the only reference she made to the party was, 'Hope you and your folks got enough to eat last night. You certainly didn't take very much. Mom never tries to figure how much food to prepare. She just puts everything on the table and hopes for the best.'

I began to relax. The Gleasons' dinner party wasn't so different from a Chinese meal after all. My mother also puts everything on the table and hopes for the best.

Meg was the first friend I had made after we came to America. I eventually got acquainted with a few other kids in school, but Meg was still the only real friend I had.

My brother didn't have any problems making friends. He spent all his time with some boys who were teaching him baseball, and in no time he could speak English much faster than I could – not better, but faster.

I worried more about making mistakes, and I spoke carefully, making sure I could say everything right before opening my mouth. At least I had a better accent than my parents, who never really got rid of their Chinese accent, even years later. My parents had both studied English in school before coming to America, but what they had studied was mostly written English, not spoken.

Father's approach to English was a scientific one. Since Chinese verbs have no tense, he was fascinated by the way English verbs changed form according to whether they were in the present, past imperfect, perfect, pluperfect, future, or future perfect tense. He was always making diagrams of verbs and their inflections, and he looked for opportunities to show off his mastery of the pluperfect and future perfect tenses, his two favorites. 'I shall have finished my project by Monday,' he would say smugly.

Mother's approach was to memorize lists of polite phrases that would cover all possible social situations. She was constantly muttering things like 'I'm fine, thank you. And you?' Once she accidentally stepped on someone's foot, and hurriedly blurted, 'Oh, that's quite all right!' Embarrassed by her slip, she resolved to do better next time. So when someone stepped on *her* foot, she cried, 'You're welcome!'

In our own different ways, we made progress in learning English. But

I had another worry, and that was my appearance. My brother didn't have to worry, since Mother bought him blue jeans for school, and he dressed like all the other boys. But she insisted that girls had to wear skirts. By the time she saw that Meg and the other girls were wearing jeans, it was too late. My school clothes were bought already, and we didn't have money left to buy new outfits for me. We had too many other things to buy first, like furniture, pots and pans.

The first time I visited Meg's house, she took me upstairs to her room, and I wound up trying on her clothes. We were pretty much the same size, since Meg was shorter and thinner than average. Maybe that's how we became friends in the first place. Wearing Meg's jeans and T-shirt, I looked at myself in the mirror. I could almost pass for an American – from the back, anyway. At least the kids in school wouldn't stop and stare at me in the hallways, which was what they did when they saw me in my white blouse and navy blue skirt that went a couple of inches below the knees.

When Meg came to my house, I invited her to try on my Chinese dresses, the ones with a high collar and slits up the sides. Meg's eyes were bright as she looked at herself in the mirror. She struck several sultry poses, and we nearly fell over laughing.

The dinner party at the Gleasons' didn't stop my growing friendship with Meg. Things were getting better for me in other ways too. Mother finally bought me some jeans at the end of the month, when Father got his paycheque. She wasn't in any hurry about buying them at first, until I worked on her. This is what I did. Since we didn't have a car in those days, I often ran down to the neighborhood store to pick up things for her. The groceries cost less at a big supermarket, but the closest one was many blocks away. One day, when she ran out of flour, I offered to borrow a bike from our neighbor's son and buy a ten-pound bag of flour at the big supermarket. I mounted the boy's bike and waved to Mother. 'I'll be back in five minutes!'

Before I started pedaling, I heard her voice behind me. 'You can't go out in public like that! People can see all the way up to your thighs!'

'I'm sorry,' I said innocently. 'I thought you were in a hurry to get the flour.' For dinner we were going to have pot-stickers (fried Chinese dumplings), and we needed a lot of flour.

'Couldn't you borrow a girl's bicycle?' complained Mother. 'That way your skirt won't be pushed up.'

'There aren't too many of those around,' I said. 'Almost all the girls wear jeans while riding a bike, so they don't see any point buying a girl's bike.'

We didn't eat pot-stickers that evening, and Mother was thoughtful. Next day we took the bus downtown and she bought me a pair of jeans. In the same week, my brother made the baseball team of his junior high school, Father started taking driving lessons, and Mother discovered rummage sales. We soon got all the furniture we needed, plus a dart board and a 1,000-piece jigsaw puzzle (fourteen hours later, we discovered that it was a 999-piece jigsaw puzzle). There was hope that the Lins might become a normal American family after all.

Then came our dinner at the Lakeview restaurant.

The Lakeview was an expensive restaurant, one of those places where a headwaiter dressed in tails conducted you to your seat, and the only light came from candles and flaming desserts. In one corner of the room a lady harpist played tinkling melodies.

Father wanted to celebrate, because he had just been promoted. He worked for an electronics company, and after his English started improving, his superiors decided to appoint him to a position more suited to his training. The promotion not only brought a higher salary but was also a tremendous boost to his pride.

Up to then we had eaten only in Chinese restaurants. Although my brother and I were becoming fond of hamburgers, my parents didn't care much for western food, other than chow mein.

But this was a special occasion, and Father asked his co-workers to recommend a really elegant restaurant. So there we were at the Lakeview, stumbling after the headwaiter in the murky dining room.

At our table we were handed our menus, and they were so big that to read mine I almost had to stand up again. But why bother? It was mostly in French, anyway.

Father, being an engineer, was always systematic. He took out a

pocket French dictionary. 'They told me that most of the items would be in French, so I came prepared.' He even had a pocket flashlight, the size of a marking pen. While Mother held the flashlight over the menu, he looked up the items that were in French.

'*Pâté en croûte*,' he muttered. 'Let's see. . . *pâté* is paste. . . *croûte* is crust. . . hmm. . . a paste in crust.'

The waiter stood looking patient. I squirmed and died at least fifty times.

At long last Father gave up. 'Why don't we just order four complete dinners at random?' he suggested.

'Isn't that risky?' asked Mother. 'The French eat some rather peculiar things, I've heard.'

'A Chinese can eat anything a Frenchman can eat,' Father declared.

The soup arrived in a plate. How do you get soup up from a plate? I glanced at the other diners, but the ones at the nearby tables were not on their soup course, while the more distant ones were invisible in the darkness.

Fortunately my parents had studied books on western etiquette before they came to America. 'Tilt your plate,' whispered my mother. 'It's easier to spoon the soup up that way.'

She was right. Tilting the plate did the trick. But the etiquette book didn't say anything about what you did after the soup reached your lips. As any respectable Chinese knows, the correct way to eat your soup is

to slurp. This helps to cool the liquid and prevent you from burning your lips. It also shows your appreciation.

We showed our appreciation. *Shloop*, went my father. *Shloop*, went my mother. *Shloop, shloop*, went my brother, who was the hungriest.

The lady harpist stopped playing to take a rest. And in the silence, our family's consumption of soup suddenly seemed unnaturally loud. You know how it sounds on a rocky beach when the tide goes out and the water drains from all those little pools? They go *shloop, shloop, shloop*. That was the Lin family, eating soup.

At the next table a waiter was pouring wine. When a large *shloop* reached him, he froze. The bottle continued to pour, and red wine flooded the tabletop and into the lap of a customer. Even the customer didn't notice anything at first, being also hypnotized by the *shloop, shloop, shloop*.

It was too much. 'I need to go to the toilet,' I mumbled, jumping to my feet. A waiter, sensing my urgency, quickly directed me to the ladies' room.

I splashed cold water on my burning face, and as I dried myself with a paper towel, I stared into the mirror. In this perfumed ladies' room, with its pink-and-silver wallpaper and marbled sinks, I looked completely out of place. What was I doing here? What was our family doing in the Lakeview restaurant? In America?

The door to the ladies' room opened. A woman came in and glanced curiously at me. I retreated into one of the toilet cubicles and latched the door.

Time passed – maybe half an hour, maybe an hour. Then I heard the door open again, and my mother's voice. 'Are you in there? You're not sick, are you?'

There was real concern in her voice. A girl can't leave her family just because they slurp their soup. Besides, the toilet cubicle had a few drawbacks as a permanent residence. 'I'm all right,' I said, undoing the latch.

Mother didn't tell me how the rest of the dinner went, and I didn't want to know. In the weeks following, I managed to push the whole thing into the back of my mind, where it jumped out at me only a few times a day. Even now, I turn hot all over when I think of the Lakeview restaurant.

But by the time we had been in this country for three months, our family was definitely making progress toward becoming Americanized. I remember my parents' first PTA meeting. Father wore a neat suit and tie, and Mother put on her first pair of high heels. She stumbled only once. They met my homeroom teacher and beamed as she told them that I would make honor roll soon at the rate I was going. Of course Chinese etiquette forced Father to say that I was a very stupid girl and Mother to protest that the teacher was showing favoritism toward me. But I could tell they were both very proud.

The day came when my parents announced that they wanted to give a dinner party. We had invited Chinese friends to eat with us before, but this dinner was going to be different. In addition to a Chinese-American family, we were going to invite the Gleasons.

'Gee, I can hardly wait to have dinner at your house,' Meg said to me. 'I just *love* Chinese food.'

That was a relief. Mother was a good cook, but I wasn't sure if people who ate sour cream would also eat chicken gizzards stewed in soy sauce.

Mother decided not to take a chance with chicken gizzards. Since we had western guests, she set the table with large dinner plates, which we never used in Chinese meals. In fact we didn't use individual plates at all, but picked up food from the platters in the middle of the table and brought it directly to our rice bowls. Following the practice of Chinese-American restaurants, Mother also placed large serving spoons on the platters.

The dinner started well. Mrs Gleason exclaimed at the beautifully arranged dishes of food: the colorful candied fruit in the sweet-and-sour pork dish, the noodle-thin shreds of chicken meat stir-fried with tiny peas, and the glistening pink prawns in a ginger sauce.

At first I was too busy enjoying my food to notice how the guests were doing. But soon I remembered my duties. Sometimes guests were too polite to help themselves and you had to serve them with more food.

I glanced at Meg, to see if she needed more food, and my eyes nearly popped out at the sight of her plate. It was piled with food: the sweet-and-sour meat pushed right against the chicken shreds, and the chicken sauce ran into the prawns. She had been taking food from a second dish before she finished eating her helping from the first!

Horrified, I turned to look at Mrs Gleason. She was dumping rice out of her bowl and putting it on her dinner plate. Then she ladled prawns and gravy on top of the rice and mixed everything together, the way you mix sand, gravel, and cement to make concrete.

I couldn't bear to look any longer, and I turned to Mr Gleason. He was chasing a pea around his plate. Several times he got it to the edge, but when he tried to pick it up with his chopsticks, it rolled back toward the center of the plate again. Finally he put down his chopsticks and picked up the pea with his fingers. He really did! A grown man!

All of us, our family and the Chinese guests, stopped eating to watch the activities of the Gleasons. I wanted to giggle. Then I caught my mother's eyes on me. She frowned and shook her head slightly, and I understood the message: the Gleasons were not used to Chinese ways, and they were just coping the best they could. For some reason I thought of celery strings.

When the main courses were finished, Mother brought out a platter of fruit. 'I hope you weren't expecting a sweet dessert,' she said. 'Since the Chinese don't eat dessert, I didn't think to prepare any.'

'Oh, I couldn't possibly eat dessert!' cried Mrs Gleason. 'I'm simply stuffed!'

Meg had different ideas. When the table was cleared, she announced that she and I were going for a walk. 'I don't know about you, but I feel like dessert,' she told me, when we were outside. 'Come on, there's a Dairy Queen down the street. I could use a big chocolate milkshake!'

Although I didn't really want anything more to eat, I insisted on paying for the milkshakes. After all, I was still hostess.

Meg got her large chocolate milkshake and I had a small one. Even so, she was finishing hers while I was only half done. Toward the end she pulled hard on her straws and went *shloop, shloop*.

'Do you always slurp when you eat a milkshake?' I asked, before I could stop myself.

Meg grinned. 'Sure. All Americans slurp.'

Lensey Namioka

Judging people

The storyteller is very aware of the way in which people judge by first impressions.

1 When you meet someone new, what influences your first impression of them?
2 How important do you think first impressions are?
3 How do you think the Gleasons judged the Lin family on the occasion of their first meal together?
4 How does the storyteller judge the Gleasons when they come to dinner at the Lins' house?

Different ways of doing things

1 What are the most important differences that the Lin family discovers between the American way of life and what they have been used to?
2 What differences have you observed in the story between American lifestyles and your own?
3 At different points in the story we are told that the Lin family is becoming Americanized. When are these and what evidence does the narrator give us of this?

Different approaches

Each member of the Lin family has a different approach to settling in America. Go through the story and make a list of how each person tackles the problems involved. You could do this in the form of a simple table, including your own comments:

Character	What she/he does	My comments
Brother	Learns baseball	A good way to make friends, and it helps him learn English.

Use the notes you have made and other points you have noticed to write short character descriptions of each member of the Lin family.

Writing

1 The story describes three meals. At two of them, the Lins are with the Gleasons. In each case we see the meal from the Lins' point of view. How do you think the Gleasons saw each meal? Write an account of each meal as one of the Gleasons might have described it:
   ● in a conversation with a friend, or
   ● in a letter to a friend, or
   ● in a personal diary.

2 The story has focused your attention on the problems faced by a newcomer to American society. Think about newcomers to your society and the problems they face. Make a story for someone of your own age, highlighting some of these problems and how the newcomer tackles them.

My grandmother

I see her now
in her wheezing gray frailty,
clutching hold of her life at the kitchen sink;
the noise of her breathing like the sound of the sea
sucking back shingle.

Woman of waves was she,
she fought back her asthma,
standing there while I grew up
and the tides came and went.

Her fingers flashed silver,
the gullie terrible in her hand.
She was at home among herring and flounders and cod.

Behind her
the crabs boiled red in the pot,
a stone on its iron lid
to keep them from crawling out
into my dreams.

Eyes that wobbled wickedly on stalks,
and claws that tore me to gobbets as I lay
drowning drowning –
she took these terrors away.

She showed me St Peter's thumb-print
on the side of the haddock.
She gave me the top of my grandfather's egg.

She washed me in the brine of her tears
that she shed nightly.

She taught me the ways of the sea.

When it was coddling and comforting I wanted, I went to my grandmother.

Out of her gray frailty she doled out kindness and warmth from kitchen and fireside, her two appointed places. She served us as if she had nothing else to do. Weak in wind and limb, she loved and protected us with the heart of a lion.

Asthma was her curse. It kept her shackled to the house all day long and all her days. It was a chain that you could hear rattling inside her, a chain forged from gray gaspings and breathlessness and wild wheezing cries. It kept her in her chair for hours at a time some days, with head bowed, her hand over her eyes, shoulders shaking, the drowning going on in her mouth as she battled for air like a spent fish.

When she was a girl of twenty her father died at sea on the way home from Yarmouth. There was no telegram to warn the family that the skipper lay dead in his boat. When she heard it was coming in, she ran down to the harbour early in the morning, waiting on the pier to welcome him, and the presents he always brought. But it was a body draped in oilskins that was brought ashore and given to her. She fled home with her grief from the sea, shut herself in the cellar, and threw herself face down on an old mattress which had lain there for years. She cried herself to sleep on that damp dismal bed, soaking it with her tears. Exhausted, she lay there till night. They couldn't rouse her, make her answer the door. Fever blazed through her for a week afterwards, and for a month or more she could scarcely walk about the house. Her constitution was ruined, a prey to asthma ever since, so the doctor said. When I was born she was barely fifty. Now I realize that she always looked eighty.

But a lifetime of illness did not harden her to the aches and ailments of other folk. She felt for them all the more sweetly. She was an expert on all the old homely cures that could never be bought from the chemist's shop. For her own asthmatic coughing bouts she used a remedy which made me gasp my lungs out to be granted just a single gulp: honey and vinegar simmered together with bruised sugar candy, and oil of sweet almonds and lemon-juice stirred in. Nectar this was, that snatched me from the imagined brink of my grave a hundred times that I can remember. These and many more medicines she soothed me with when I felt like being ill. She held my head when I banged it hard against the sides of the whirling world; she cleaned my cuts and wiped my nose; she warmed my bed with the big stone hot water bottle, always wrapping it round twice with a towel so that it would not burn my toes. And when I came in dirty, she stripped me and plunged me into the big bubbling kitchen sink, beating the blackness out of me with bars of carbolic, rubbing me down in front of the fire until I was pink and tingling and resurrected.

Still when I think of her, she is the provider, flooding the kitchen with waves of rich aromas from her plain and wholesome fare. Kail and potatoes were the staple diet, with the mutton removed from the soup to serve as the second course along with mash. Or she turned the tatties into a meal in themselves by beating them in with turnips and onions and lashings of pepper, whipping them into an explosive mixture which she called clapshot. Or she used dripping and a little sausage meat instead, and the tatties were turned into stovies. The simple wooden chapper and spurtle were the tools that worked the magic, and the results were served up on the faded azure background of willow-patterned bowls and plates and dishes – mild-mouthed monks and love-lipped ladies, serene and sedate by their blue-leafed pools and bowered bridges, bowing to their pig-tailed lords; fanning themselves from the heat of our scalding hot meals, faded lords and ladies; faded but never fading throughout the twelve eternal years of my childhood.

Bannocks and baps and loaves of crusty bread came out of the side-ovens, heated by the fire – she baked for us when we could not afford to buy from Mrs Guthrie. But more than anything I recall how she worked her way through endless quantities of fish. The king of fish, the humble herring, became in her hands the fish for a king. She boiled them, fried them in oatmeal, roasted them on the brander, dished them up as kippers, as bufters, as bloaters, shredded them into hairy potatoes; producing variety out of monotony. Herrings and haddocks and cod she fed us on – and shoals of flatfish to be picked to the bone.

They were brought to the house in bunches of six or twelve, knotted together, the twine threaded through their tough, gaping mouths. Dangling like bells from my grandfather's crooked finger, jangling inside my head out of their silvery silence, their tails sweeping the pathway as he strode through the door, slapping them heavily into the sink. Grandmother wrenched off their heads, she from whose gentle heart pity ran so soon. She threw them through the open window to the hysterical gulls and the sniffing cats. She cut off their tails and slit open their bellies with her terrible flashing knife. The dark red slivers fell out, desecrated, like wounds on display. She ripped off the scaly sheen of their skins just as my auntie Jenny peeled off her nylons without thought. She stripped them quietly of death's last dignities, dumb brutes of the sea, boning them till they were nothing more than flabby slabs of fresh white meat – the quicksilver of the sea brought down to earth so that we might eat. *Mare vivimus*. We live by the sea.

So she stood there at her kitchen sink long hours at a time, stood there while the tides came and went, her menfolk going out and coming home, the years passing as she grew older without ageing. Sometimes she paused, the knife slippery in her still hand, fighting away her asthma. I looked at her in wonder – the bowed, beaten back, bent with the stripes of pointless suffering, the mouth opening and shutting in the same silent agony as the fish she waited patiently to dress for death's dismemberment. She laid her hands on my shoulders for a few minutes at a time, and we stood together in silence, each of us incapable of finding words.

Then she carried on patiently. She taught me how to gut and fillet. She showed me St Peter's thumb-mark on the side of the haddock – and now, alas, in this age of frozen food in plastic packets, my fishfingers have become indeed all thumbs.

But it is the crabs that remain – crawling horribly into the present. The big partan crabs were brought into the house looking like fallen knights, their armour-gauntleted claws folded quietly on their bellies as if they were dead and laid to rest. But when they were picked up they sprang to attention, opening their claws wide and waiting for the attack, to clutch and pierce and tear. Grandmother had no fear of them and laughed at the panic that sent me to the other side of the kitchen. She dropped them into the pot on the grate, holding them round the back, where the blind, waving pincers could not grip her. Horrified, I watched the water begin to boil, and the crabs crimsoning in the agonies of death, the claws now gripping grimly onto the rim of the pot as they tried to vault their way to escape, to joust with me on the kitchen floor.

It was then that I screamed.

'Gran, they're getting out!'

It was probably for my benefit that she put on the heavy iron lid, with a stone placed on top to prevent this armed escape and a scarlet revenge. But still they come scrabbling out of the pot and into my dreams, those crabs that dined on sailors, all bubbling and bulging and red with rage and terror. Could a merciful stiletto not have been inserted between the joints of these armoured plates, to reach the vital parts and deliver a quick kill? Or to still the beating of that brutal brain. I imagined grandmother's knitting needle used in the manner of a misericorde on a medieval field. But she who was so pitiful told me that they must be boiled alive. And so, having failed to secure mercy for them, I dreamt again of those demon faces that would be visiting the sins of the grandmothers upon the children down the generations; starting in sleep with myself, with punishing infestations of eyes that wobbled wickedly on stalks, and claws that tore me to gobbets where I lay. For a time they made night hideous.

Christopher Rush

First impressions

After reading the story for the first time, what are your first impressions of:
1 The time and place where it is set
2 The way of life of the people who live there
3 The grandmother
4 The writer as a small boy?

Thinking about character

Now focus on the way in which the character of the grandmother is described in the story.
1 Read it again. Find out about these aspects of her character and make some notes:
   a) the main events of her life
   b) her asthma
   c) her skills as a cook
   d) how she treated the narrator as a small boy.
2 Discuss these with a partner or in a group.
3 Add to your notes.
4 Now write a description of the grandmother's character.

Story and poem

Most of what is in the poem is also in the story. You can see this if you compare the first two verses of the poem with two paragraphs from the story:

I see her now
in her wheezing gray frailty,
clutching hold of her life at the kitchen
     sink;
the noise of her breathing like the
     sound of the sea
sucking back shingle.

Woman of waves was she,
she fought back her asthma,
standing there while I grew up
and the tides came and went.

As you can see, the subject matter is the same and certain words and phrases from the story also occur in the poem:

asthma
wheezing
gray
at . . . kitchen sink
the tides came and went

The way in which they have been selected and ordered is different. Read the poem and story again and find other parallels like this. What do you think are the most important differences between the two?

Asthma was her curse. It kept her shackled to the house all day long and all her days. It was a chain that you could hear rattling inside her, a chain forged from gray gaspings and breathlessness and wild wheezing cries. It kept her in her chair for hours at a time some days, with head bowed, her hand over her eyes, shoulders shaking, the drowning going on in her mouth as she battled for air like a spent fish.

So she stood there at her kitchen sink long hours at a time, stood there while the tides came and went, her menfolk going out and coming home, the years passing as she grew older without ageing. Sometimes she paused, the knife slippery in her still hand, fighting away her asthma. I looked at her in wonder – the bowed, beaten back, bent with the stripes of pointless suffering, the mouth opening and shutting in the same silent agony as the fish she waited patiently to dress for death's dismemberment. She laid her hands on my shoulders for a few minutes at a time, and we stood together in silence, each of us incapable of finding words.

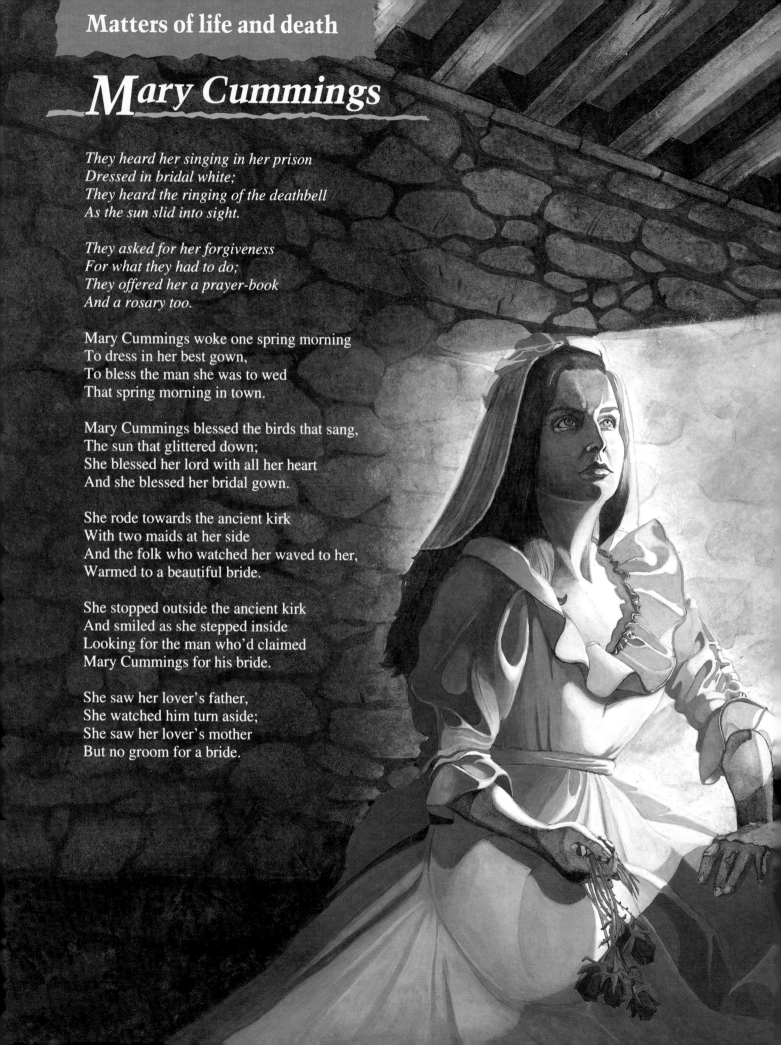

Mary Cummings

They heard her singing in her prison
Dressed in bridal white;
They heard the ringing of the deathbell
As the sun slid into sight.

They asked for her forgiveness
For what they had to do;
They offered her a prayer-book
And a rosary too.

Mary Cummings woke one spring morning
To dress in her best gown,
To bless the man she was to wed
That spring morning in town.

Mary Cummings blessed the birds that sang,
The sun that glittered down;
She blessed her lord with all her heart
And she blessed her bridal gown.

She rode towards the ancient kirk
With two maids at her side
And the folk who watched her waved to her,
Warmed to a beautiful bride.

She stopped outside the ancient kirk
And smiled as she stepped inside
Looking for the man who'd claimed
Mary Cummings for his bride.

She saw her lover's father,
She watched him turn aside;
She saw her lover's mother
But no groom for a bride.

Mary Cummings cursed that father,
She wished that old man blind
So that sad old man would never see
The pain in Mary's mind.

Mary Cummings cursed that mother,
For bearing such a child
Who could leave Mary Cummings in her bridal gown
Abandoned and defiled.

The mother slithered to the ground,
The father's eyes went white;
Mary called on hell to hound their son
And to claim his soul that night.

She cursed at their forgiveness,
She praised what they had to do;
She threw aside their prayer-book
And their rosary too.

She kept on singing in her prison
As the sun slid out of sight
And prepared for her dark new lover
In her bridal gown of white.

Alan Bold

Clues

The poem is full of hints about the background to the story and about what is happening. Make a list of all the clues you can find and then try to answer these questions:

What do you think has happened?
What do you think is about to happen?

Once you feel you understand the story, imagine that Mary Cummings has one final chance to share her story and her feelings with a friend. She asks that friend to write it all down so that it will not be lost. What does she tell her?

Pretty Boy Floyd

Come and gather 'round me, children,
A story I will tell
About Pretty Boy Floyd, the outlaw,
Oklahoma knew him well.

It was in the town of Shawnee
On a Saturday afternoon,
His wife beside him in the wagon,
As into town they rode.

There a deputy sheriff approached him
In a manner rather rude,
Using vulgar words of anger,
And his wife, she overheard.

Pretty Boy grabbed a log chain,
The deputy grabbed his gun,
And in the fight that followed
He laid that deputy down.

Then he took to the trees and the timber
To live a life of shame,
Every crime in Oklahoma
Was added to his name.

Yes, he took to the river bottom
Along the river shore,
And Pretty Boy found a welcome
At every farmer's door.

The paper said that Pretty Boy
Had robbed a bank each day,
While he was sitting in some farmhouse,
Three hundred miles away.

There's many a starving farmer
The same old story told,
How the outlaw paid their mortgage
And saved their little home.

Others tell you 'bout a stranger
That come to beg a meal,
And underneath his napkin
Left a thousand-dollar bill.

It was in Oklahoma City,
It was on a Christmas Day,
There came a whole carload of groceries
With a note to say:

'You say that I'm an outlaw,
You say that I'm a thief,
Here's a Christmas dinner
For the families on relief.'

Yes, as through this world I've rambled
I've seen lots of funny men,
Some will rob you with a six gun,
And some with a fountain pen.

But as through your life you travel,
Wherever you may roam,
You won't never see no outlaw
Drive a family from their home.

Woodie Guthrie

Modern ballads

Both these poems can be described as ballads: poems that have short verses in a regular pattern, and that tell a story. Ballads go back hundreds of years, but the form is still used by poets and song-writers today. Both these ballads are based on true stories about real people, and the poets have used the facts to express deeply held beliefs.

The facts

Read each ballad carefully and work out the facts that each one contains. Make a list of them. Against each fact, note the number of the line(s) where you found it.

The bad guys

Each of these poems has its 'good guys' and its 'bad guys'. Think about each poem again. Who exactly are the bad guys in each poem, and why?

88

Ballad of sixty-five

The roads are rocky and the hills are steep,
The macca scratches and the gully's deep.
The town is far, news travels slow.
And the mountain men have far to go.

Bogle took his cutlass at Stony Gut
And looked at the small heap of food he'd got
And he shook his head, and his thoughts were sad,
'You can wuk like a mule but de crop still bad'.

Bogle got his men and he led them down
Over the hills to Spanish Town.
They chopped their way and they made a track
To the Governor's house. But he sent them back.

As they trudged home back to Stony Gut
Paul's spirit sank with each bush he cut,
For he thought of the hungry St Thomas men
Who were waiting for the message he'd bring to
   them.

They couldn't believe that he would fail
And their anger rose when they heard his tale.
Then they told Paul Bogle of Morant Bay
And the poor man fined there yesterday.

Then Bogle thundered, 'This thing is wrong.
They think we weak, but we hill men strong.
Rouse up yourself. We'll march all night
To the Vestry house, and we'll claim our right.'

The Monday morning was tropic clear
As the men from Stony Gut drew near,
Clenching their sticks in their farmer's hand
To claim their rights in their native land.

Oh many mourned and many were dead
That day when the vestry flames rose red.
There was chopping and shooting and when it done
Paul Bogle and his men knew they had to run.

They ran for the bush where they hoped to hide
But the soldiers poured in from Kingston side.
They took their prisoners to Morant Bay
Where they hanged them high in the early day.

Paul Bogle died but his spirit talks
Anywhere in Jamaica that freedom walks,
Where brave men gather and courage thrills
As it did in those days in St Thomas hills.

Alma Norman

The beliefs

Once you know who the good guys and the bad
guys are, you can start to work out the writer's
beliefs that lie beneath the poem. Think about
this:
1 How would you sum up each writer's beliefs
   as expressed in the poem?
2 Can you find a few lines from each that
   express these beliefs vividly?
3 What are your opinions about the beliefs
   expressed?

Popular hero

Each poem describes a person who was a popular hero in his own time and among his own
people. Can you think of any popular heroes
from your own time, who might become the
subject of a similar ballad? What qualities do
they show that make them popular heroes?

A different kind of courage

Albie Sachs was arrested and imprisoned by the South African Government because he supported the African National Congress. In his Prison Diary *he recorded what it was like to be kept in prison.*

'Constable, would it be possible for me to get clean blankets sent in from outside? These are quite warm, but they're filled with fleas.'

The constable puts my food on the floor and, as he straightens up, looks at the blankets to which I am referring.

'What's wrong with the powder we used?' He sounds offended.

'Well, it doesn't seem to have had any effect on the fleas, but it nearly kills me,' I reply. 'As soon as I lie down I start sneezing. My eyes water and I can't breathe properly. I have to have a handkerchief over my nose when I try to sleep.'

'You'll have to ask the sergeant.'

'When will I see him?'

'He'll come this evening.'

'Thank you constable. I'll ask the sergeant.'

At intermittent moments in the afternoon I repeat to myself that I must ask the sergeant about the blankets. If only I could write it down. Eventually the sergeant comes, asks if I am all right, and leaves . . . I forgot to ask him. I keep on forgetting the simplest things. I must, I must, I must remember tomorrow.

'Sergeant, would it be possible for me to get clean blankets from outside? The flea powder in these is worse than the fleas. I meant to ask you yesterday, but I forgot.'

'You'll have to ask the station commander.'

'When will I see him?'

'He holds an inspection on Sunday before he goes to church.'

'Thank you, sergeant. I'll ask him then.'

The neat grey suit he is wearing makes the station commander look smaller than he does when he is in uniform. My door is open and the ringing of the church bells is no longer muffled. Standing with the station commander are two young boys also dressed in their Sunday best. Before setting off for church they are accompanying Pa to look at his prison and the new prisoners. Today I won't forget. How does one address a station commander? I suppose 'Mr' is best.

'Mr Kruger, would it be possible for clean blankets to be sent in to me from outside? These are full of fleas, I'm afraid. Your men have very kindly tried using insect powder, but it doesn't seem to affect the fleas at all. My clothing is all bloody from the bites, and I'm sure my mother can arrange for some new blankets to be sent in.'

The station commander is a man who carries out his instructions with neither special humanity nor special harshness. He is terse, colourless and efficient, but today, perhaps with a view to impressing on his sons how 'firm but just' he is, his reply actually runs to a few sentences.

'We do the best we can to keep the blankets clean,' he tells me, 'but you must realize it is very difficult, especially bearing in mind most of the prisoners we have. I am not allowed to let you have anything from outside except food and clothes, so there's nothing I can do.'

90

'But aren't blankets the same as clothes really?' I ask.

'My instructions only speak about clothes, not blankets. You had better ask the security men when they next come. They will have to decide.'

'If they give permission will you make the arrangement with my mother?'

'Yes, but only if they give permission.'

The first time the security men come I forget to ask them. Again I feel chagrin at the inability of my mind to hold such a simple idea.

The door opens and the two lieutenants are there. When they ask me how I am, I tell them about the blankets. 'The station commander said that if you did not oppose it, he would make all the arrangements,' I conclude.

'When you answer questions things will be much better for you. Then you can ask us for what you want.'

'But this has nothing to do with whether I answer questions or not. Every prisoner has the right to certain civilized standards, no matter why he is being held.

'There's nothing we can do about it. Only Pretoria can authorize it.'

'Pretoria, you mean my simple request has to go all the way to police headquarters in Pretoria? Surely they can leave a little thing like this to you people down here. Well, if that's the case, will you send on my request to Pretoria?'

'Our job is to question you, not to worry about your facilities.'

'Well, who can I ask then?'

'Ask the magistrate when he comes round. He has the direct ear of the Minister. If anyone can fix it up for you, he is the one. Ask him.'

Until now the magistrate has not been very helpful. He was only recently transferred to Cape Town so I have never appeared before him in Court. I am sure the other magistrates would not have been as harsh. When I told him of the warrant officer who on the day of my arrest had sharpened a pocket knife in front of me and told me, 'You know what this is for, don't you?' the magistrate's only reaction was to tell me the officer was probably only joking. These inspections which he has to do once a week are obviously very tiresome to him.

As the cell door opens I see him standing with pencil poised ready to tick off my name.

'Have you any complaints?' he asks briefly.

'Yes, I'm being bitten to pieces by fleas. I can't sleep at night and my clothes are all bloody. I'd like some clean blankets from outside. There's no question of security involved. The security branch men said I should ask you.'

'Blankets are not in my department. . .'

Albie Sachs

The other time

He killed a man
In a drunken brawl
They tried him, hanged him.
That was all.

But he left his wife
Nearly penniless
She was raven-haired,
She was glamorous,

She had swooned in court,
She had caused a stir.
And the editor of
The 'Sunday Blare',

Aware of his readers'
Appetite
And judging she should
Be worth a bit

Hired a snooper
Round to her house
With an offer she thought
Quite fabulous.

If she'd lend her picture,
Lend her name
To a story about
Her life with Him

They'd write it up
From what she said
Did she understand?
She understood.

'I've never had much.
I've still less now,
I need the money.
The answer's "no".'

As he rose to go
He noticed a medal,
Mounted and framed,
Above the mantel.

And asked her about it
Where was it won?
When did he get it?
What had he done?

'Oh, that,' she said.
'They pinned that on
The other time
He killed a man.'

Peter Appleton

This is. . .

Each one of these statements could be a description of what the poem is about.

1 Think of at least one reason to support each of the statements.
2 Which do you think is the most important statement and why?
3 Make up one more statement (number 6) to add to the list.
4 How would you rank all six statements in order of their importance to the poem?

1 This is a story about newspapers.
2 This is a story about capital punishment.
3 This is a story about the morality of killing.
4 This is a story about the evil use of money.
5 This is a story about what money cannot buy.
6 This is a story about...

The facts

1 Read the poem again and make a list of the facts that you can discover about the man and his wife.
2 Which of these facts do you think are relevant to a newspaper story?
3 Which of these facts do you think are likely to be used in a newspaper story?

4 What else might a journalist want to know? Imagine that you worked for the newspaper. Make a list of the questions that you might put together before visiting the woman to interview her.

The interview

1 How do you imagine the interview went between the journalist and the hanged man's wife?
2 How do you imagine the characters of the journalist and the woman?
3 How might the journalist have treated her?
4 What sort of questions would he have asked?
5 What sort of answers would she have given?

Now make up your version of the interview.
Either:
1 Work with a partner and do a role play of the conversation; or
2 Write it as a script. (See page 178.)

Thinking further

1 How is the woman in the poem described and treated?
2 What are your feelings about this?
3 Peter Appleton probably gave the newspaper an imaginary name so that he could not be sued for libel. In which newspaper(s) would you expect to find this kind of story?
4 Why do you think people like reading this kind of story?

The case for the defence

It was the strangest murder trial I ever attended. They named it 'The Peckham Murder' in the headlines, though Northwood Street, where the old woman was found battered to death, was not strictly speaking in Peckham. This was not one of those cases of circumstantial evidence in which you feel the jurymen's anxiety – because mistakes have been made – like domes of silence muting the court. No, this murderer was all but found with the body; no one present when the Crown counsel outlined his case believed that the man in the dock stood any chance at all.

He was a heavy stout man with bulging, bloodshot eyes. All his muscles seemed to be in his thighs. Yes, an ugly customer, one you wouldn't forget in a hurry – and that was an important point because the Crown proposed to call four witnesses who hadn't forgotten him, who had seen him hurrying away from the little red villa in Northwood Street. The clock had just struck two in the morning.

Mrs Salmon in 15 Northwood Street had been unable to sleep; she heard a door click shut and thought it was her own gate. So she went to the window and saw Adams (that was his name) on the steps of Mrs Parker's house. He had just come out and he was wearing gloves. He had a hammer in his hand and she saw him drop it into the laurel bushes by the front gate. But before he moved away, he had looked up – at her window. The fatal instinct that tells a man when he is watched exposed him in the light of a street-lamp to her gaze – his eyes suffused with horrifying and brutal fear, like an animal's when you raise a whip.
I talked afterwards to Mrs Salmon, who naturally after the astonishing verdict went in fear herself. As I imagine did all the witnesses – Henry MacDougall, who had been driving home from Benfleet late and nearly ran Adams down at the corner of Northwood Street. Adams was walking in the middle of the road looking dazed. And old Mr Wheeler, who lived next door to Mrs Parker, at No. 12, and was wakened by a noise – like a chair falling – through the thin-as-paper villa wall, and got up and looked out of the window, just as Mrs Salmon had done, saw Adams's back and, as he turned, those bulging eyes. In Laurel Avenue he had been seen by yet another witness – his luck was badly out; he might as well have committed the crime in broad daylight.

'I understand,' counsel said, 'that the defence proposes to plead mistaken identity. Adams's wife will tell you that he was with her at two in the morning on February 14, but after you have heard the witnesses for the Crown and examined carefully the features of the prisoner, I do not think you will be prepared to admit the possibility of a mistake.' It was all over, you would have said, but the hanging.

After the formal evidence had been given by the policeman who had found the body and the surgeon who examined it, Mrs Salmon was called. She was the ideal witness, with her slight Scotch accent and her expression of honesty, care and kindness.

The counsel for the Crown brought the story gently out. She spoke very firmly. There was no malice in her, and no sense of importance at standing there in the Central Criminal Court with a judge in scarlet hanging on her words and the reporters writing them down. Yes, she said, and then she had gone downstairs and rung up the police station.

'And do you see the man here in court?'

She looked straight at the big man in the dock, who stared hard at her with his pekingese eyes without emotion.

'Yes,' she said, 'there he is.'

'You are quite certain?'

She said simply, 'I couldn't be mistaken, sir.'

It was all as easy as that.

'Thank you, Mrs Salmon.'

Counsel for the defence rose to cross-examine. If you had reported as many murder trials as I have, you would have known beforehand what line he would take. And I was right, up to a point.

'Now, Mrs Salmon, you must remember that a man's life may depend on your evidence.'

'I do remember it, sir.'

'Is your eyesight good?'

'I have never had to wear spectacles, sir.'

'You are a woman of fifty-five?'

'Fifty-six, sir.'

'And the man you saw was on the other side of the road?'

'Yes, sir.'

'And it was two o'clock in the morning. You must have remarkable eyes, Mrs Salmon?'

'No, sir. There was moonlight, and when the man looked up, he had the lamplight on his face.'

'And you have no doubt whatever that the man you saw is the prisoner?'

I couldn't make out what he was at. He couldn't have expected any other answer than the one he got.

'None whatever, sir. It isn't a face one forgets.'

Counsel took a look round the court for a moment. Then he said, 'Do you mind, Mrs Salmon, examining again the people in court? No, not the prisoner. Stand up, please Mr Adams,' and there at the back of the court with thick stout body and muscular legs and a pair of bulging eyes, was the exact image of the man in the dock. He was even dressed the same – tight blue suit and striped tie.

'Now think very carefully, Mrs Salmon. Can you still swear that the man you saw drop the hammer in Mrs Parker's garden was the prisoner – and not this man who is his twin brother?'

Of course she couldn't. She looked from one to the other and didn't say a word.

There the big brute sat in the dock with his legs crossed and there he stood too at the back of the court and they both stared at Mrs Salmon.

She shook her head.

What we saw then was the end of the case. There wasn't a witness prepared to swear that it was the prisoner he'd seen. And the brother? He had his alibi too; he was with his wife.

And so the man was acquitted for lack of evidence. But whether – if he did the murder and not his brother – he was punished or not, I don't know. That extraordinary day had an extraordinary end. I followed Mrs Salmon out of court and we got wedged in the crowd who were waiting, of course, for the twins. The police tried to draw the crowd away, but all they could do was keep the roadway clear for traffic. I learned later that they tried to get the twins to leave by a back way, but they wouldn't. One of them – no one knew which – said, 'I've been acquitted, haven't I?' and they walked bang out of the front entrance. Then it happened. I don't know how, though I was only six feet away. The crowd moved and somehow one of the twins got pushed on the road right in front of a bus.

He gave a squeal like a rabbit and that was all; he was dead, his skull smashed just as Mrs Parker's had been. Divine vengeance? I wish I knew. There was the other Adams getting on his feet from beside the body and looking straight over at Mrs Salmon. He was crying, but whether he was the murderer or the innocent man nobody will ever be able to tell. But if you were Mrs Salmon, could you sleep at night?

Graham Greene

Another story

1 Suppose it was the *innocent* brother who was killed and the murderer was left to 'tell the tale'. Tell the story of the trial and what happened after it as if you were the murderer talking to one of his friends.

2 Suppose it was the *murderer* who was killed and the innocent brother was left to 'tell the tale'. Tell the story of the trial and what happened after it as if you were the innocent brother talking to a member of the family.

One question from a bullet

I want to give up being a bullet
I've been a bullet too long

I want to be an innocent coin
in the hand of a child
and be squeezed through the slot
of a bubblegum machine

I want to give up being a bullet
I've been a bullet too long

I want to be a good luck seed
lying idle in somebody's pocket
or some ordinary little stone
on the way to becoming an earring
or just lying there unknown
among a crowd of other ordinary stones

I want to give up being a bullet
I've been a bullet too long

The question is
Can you give up being a killer?

John Agard

The difference

A knife, now, for good or ill
snugly serves the hands of skill:
whittles a whistle, carves a name,
flies at a throw to the thrower's aim;
it slices ham, it skins a goat,
scrapes a carrot, or cuts a throat.
Your right hand marries some kind of knife
for better or worse the most of your life.

But a gun was fashioned for no other skill
and no other purpose than aiming to kill.

Gloria Rawlinson

*T*ough guy

There's a tear trying to tiptoe
towards the edge of your eye tough guy
there's a tear leaning
in the direction of your eye
towards the rim of your eye tough guy

What's the matter tough guy

Why do you push it down
with the palm of your ego

A tear wouldn't bruise your eyelid

Maybe tough guy when you were a kid
they told you little boys don't cry
Didn't you ever see your Daddy peeling onions?

Your hands can talk to steel and batteries
but can't bear to deal
with the weight of a leaf

Tough luck tough guy
have a good cry

John Agard

Comparisons

The difference/One question from a bullet

1 What is the attitude of each poem towards guns and bullets?
2 Each poem makes comparisons. How do these work in each case?
3 The poems have different shapes. *The difference* uses rhymes, while *One question from a bullet* doesn't, but is divided into three main sections, each of which starts 'I want to give up being a bullet'. How does the shape affect your enjoyment and understanding of the poem?
4 Which poem do you prefer and why?

Tough guy/One question from a bullet

Compare these two poems.
Think about each of these topics:

1 The narrator of each poem
2 The style of each poem
3 How each poem ends
4 The message of each poem.

The flashlight

Next to having a revolver (which of course you could never get; which you would never really *want*; which, nevertheless, it was always pleasant to imagine you wanted more than anything else in the world), having a flashlight was a wonderful thing.

You could never have a revolver because you might make a mistake with it and kill a friend instead of Mr Davis, the principal of Emerson School. You might not be accurate with the thing and you might shoot off somebody's nose. Somebody nice, standing on the corner, at high noon, with his hand over where his nose had been, and your heart full of regret, and your mouth trying to say, 'Honest, Mr Wheeler, I didn't mean to shoot your nose off. I was shooting at that chicken-hawk flying over the roof of the Republican Building. I'm sorry, Mr Wheeler. I apologise.'

Or you might get bawled up, trying to take a quick second shot at the circling chicken-hawk, turn quickly, and shoot off your own nose.

It was the same with a horse, too.

Unpredictable.

A flashlight was another story.

Your sick cousin Joe's real name was Hovsep. Hovsep is Joseph in Armenian. Like yourself, Joe was eleven years old, only funnier. A month and a half younger, too. Which means that – well, you were first. You were ahead of him. You arrived a month and a half before he did.

So you went in and asked his mother how he was and tears came to her eyes, and she said, 'I don't know. The doctor's with him.'

You went out to the street, into the darkness of November, and began to walk home. You wished you had the revolver and the horse, so you could jump on the horse and go galloping over the streets, and draw the revolver, and do something swift and reckless to make Joe get better.

The whole thing was a mistake. Joe had no business being sick with the flu, and if he died – well, by God, you'd get even. 'If Joe dies,' you said on the way home, 'you'll get yours.' It was a clear cold night and it was the greatest time in the world to be alive, with many wonderful years of adventure ahead.

You were too busy being sore about Joe to remember how scared you were of the dark, and then all of a sudden you remembered. For a minute you were real scared, and then you pressed your thumb down on the button of the flashlight, and the light went on, and you weren't scared any more. So you flashed the light around; to the ground; up into the branches of trees; left and right; north and south. And then suddenly, as you walked, it was all over, Joe was dead, you were walking down the street alone, the years were gone, it was a night in November again many years later, and you were still sore and you still couldn't believe it. You flashed the light to the trunk of a tree and said, 'Joe?' But nobody was there. And a moment later you turned the light to the dark

100

steps of a porch, thinking he might be sitting there, and you said, 'Joe?'
But he wasn't there, either.

The next day you couldn't wait to run over to Joe's during lunch hour.
When the noon bell rang, you jumped out of your desk, got to the door
first, got out of the building first, and began running up L Street, down
San Benito Avenue, until you got tired and couldn't run any more.
'Please,' you said. 'Please don't let Joe die.' You got out the flashlight
and turned it on, but the daylight was brighter than the light of the
flashlight, and you could see everything, so what good was a flashlight
now? You kept hurrying and flashing the light at everything, as if it
were night, as if Joe was in the last night of life, and you were looking
for him, and you kept asking the question: 'Joe?'

At last you got to the house and stood on the sidewalk and looked at
it. Was it a house that had a dead boy in it named Joe? Was it a house
full of the amazed, sorrowing mothers and fathers, grandmothers and
grandfathers, great-grandmothers and great-grandfathers of Joe
Hagopian, the eleven-year-old American whose family arrived
seventeen years ago from Bitlis? Did the house contain the living and
the dead of a tribe just cheated of its son?

You went to the back door, quietly into the kitchen, and saw his
mother, and you knew from her face that the light from the flashlight
had found God's heart in the darkness of the November night, and in the
brightness of the November day, and you knew Joe was alive, with the
heart of God beating in him. And you knew that that great heart would
go on beating in him all the years that had roared by your ears the night
before. You knew the dead grandmothers and grandfathers were all
smiling, and you didn't say anything. You just looked up at Joe's
mother and smiled.

'He's all right now,' she said. 'He'll be up in a few days. Come back
after school. Maybe he'll be awake.'

'Sure,' you said. 'Here, when he wakes up, give him this flashlight.
He can flash it on in the night at the walls and the ceiling. Mighty fine
invention.'

William Saroyan

Mary Cummings

The poem mentions several characters in the story apart from Mary Cummings:
- her lover
- her lover's father
- her lover's mother

Put each of them in the hot seat and question them about their part in the story and their thoughts and feelings about Mary's execution.

Pretty Boy Floyd

Imagine that two middle-aged parents are talking to each other about the weather and the subject of Pretty Boy Floyd crops up. One of them believes all the bad things that are said about him whilst the other has the opposite view. Do a pair role play based on what they say to each other.

Ballad of sixty-five

Prepare a group reading of this poem:
1 Think about how you want to interpret the poem; the effects you want to achieve in your reading.
2 Decide how you will arrange it. Think about:
   - the number of readers
   - how the lines should be shared between the readers and why
   - whether any lines should be read by more than one reader.
3 Decide who in the group will read which parts.
4 Practise your reading.

A different kind of courage

Think about the story

1 How many different people does Albie Sachs ask about the blankets?
2 What reason does each give for not being able to help?
3 Why do you think they all refuse to help?
4 What does this story tell you about the prison and the people who run it?

Writing

Albie Sachs wrote:

> 'About one thing I have never at any stage had any doubts and that was that I have been locked up not for being bad, but for being good.'

Imagine that this had happened to you – you have been locked up for being good. Decide what it is that you have done and why you did it. Imagine what it is like as you are locked into your cell for the first time. Write about your thoughts and feelings.

The case for the defence

Conversations

The end of the court case, and what happened after, must have given people subjects for conversation for a long time. Different people would have found different parts of the story important.

Work with a partner, or in a group of four, and improvise these conversations:

- the judge and a lawyer friend
- Mrs Salmon and a friend
- the defence and prosecution lawyers
- the prosecution lawyer and the journalist who wrote the story
- two members of the jury

The flashlight

1 What is unusual about the way in which this story is told?
2 Why do you think the writer does this?
3 What does it tell us about the storyteller, his life, and the way he thinks?
4 Exactly what happened:
   17 years ago
   11 years ago
   One November evening
   The following day.
5 What is the importance of each of these:
   a revolver
   a horse
   a flashlight.
6 What is so important about the storyteller giving the flashlight to Joe?

General assignments

1 Newspapers

Many of the poems and stories in this unit involve incidents that are likely to have been reported by daily newspapers. Choose one of them and prepare the front page story that a newspaper might have run about the events described in it. You may invent the extra details that you would need for your story.

2 Justice

1 Many of these poems and stories have something to say about justice. Which ones do?
2 What is it in each of the situations that you feel is unjust or unfair?
3 Which situation angered you most?
4 Which made you think most deeply?
5 Try to explain how these stories and poems have influenced your views on punishment.

Part B

Using words

Conditions of service

There is no way that you can advertise paper rounds until you know what you are advertising. We think these are the main questions.

What time will people be expected to start?

How many houses will there be in each round?

Should all rounds be the same length?

What about sickness and holidays?

Should morning and evening rounds be separated?

Are morning rounds worth a bigger wage than weekday rounds?

What do you need to pay for the rounds you have planned?

Remember that you have to make a profit but you also have to keep your staff.

I think people who get up in the morning deserve a medal as well as a salary.

I reckon that smaller rounds for more people make sense.

You need to be flexible if you want to attract people.

Most people need the money and want a decent-sized round.

Advertising

Classified advertisements are cheapest but you cannot say very much and your one tends to get lost amongst the others.

HARMONY COSMETICS require consultants. Tel (287) 836432

PART TIME FLOOR CLEANER required, Haygarth area six mornings 7.45-9.00 wages £18 Tel: 826 91674

The bigger the advertisement the better it is ... but it also costs more.

BRANSDON HALL HOTEL
needs
part-time bar staff
top rates
tel Bransdon 283654

NEED EXTRA MONEY?

Let us train you to join our team of part time canvassers.

Telephone Bransdon 19437
(Evenings or weekends)

URGENT
EXPERIENCED SILVER SERVICE WAITERS/WAITRESSES
needed by busy catering recruitment agency
Good working conditions
Excellent rates of pay
Why not give us a ring?
**CALL ANTHEA AT
BRANSDON CATERING SERVICES
279 56297**

This is the absolute maximum size we can afford.

Let's write down everything we need to say.

The ad can be simple. We can say more when people apply.

Decision time

After talking it through, come to a decision about:

1 How much it is worth spending on advertising.
2 How you are going to advertise.
3 What your advert will say.
4 On radio: what it will sound like.
5 In the paper: what it will look like.

Making the appointments

Well, we advertised the jobs and this is the response we had. Now we have got to make the appointments.

Carla Watts aged 10

Showed enthusiasm when responding to the advertisement and says her father would bring her in every morning. Has not had any kind of job before.

Mohammed Naseem aged 15

Has a bicycle. His school have described him as a non-attender. Often works in a shop owned by a family friend during the day.

Jeanette Harding aged 14

Wrote a polite and impressive application. Used to work as a cleaner and the firm have given her a good reference. Has admitted in her letter that she has a conviction for shoplifting.

Sarah Khan aged 14

Has said she would like a round but that she does not think her father will allow her to work in the dark. Used to work in a take-away but left after two months.

Tracy Fenton aged 14

Only wants an evening round. Has said that she needs money to save for her holidays. Has not worked before.

Mr John Kirkpatrick aged 62

Retired early and wants part time work. Used to be an inspector on the buses. Has a problem with arthritis but says he is able to do the job.

Elizabeth Curtis/ Michelle Harris aged 13

Have applied to share one of the jobs. Say that they will come to their own arrangements about who does what.

Paul Ogunsanya aged 16

His command of English is poor as he has only lived in this country for four months. Seems keen and is not involved in examinations because of his recent arrival here.

Dean Bortega aged 19

Unemployed at present. Admits that he is looking for a full time job. Had been on a youth training programme but left saying that it was no good.

Simon Morgan aged 12

Says that he would have a go at a paper round although he would really like to work in the shop. Used to do car cleaning on Saturdays around Milton Street but gave it up.

Interviewing

We want to be fair to people but we don't feel we've got the time to interview everyone. These are the questions on which we think we need to reach an agreement.

What kind of person do we need for these rounds?

What questions do we need to ask the people we interview?

Who shall we choose to see?

Who do we think we are most likely to appoint if they are reasonable in the interview?

Do we need to consider changing the rounds that are on offer in order to attract the people we want?

The survey

You are going to conduct a small-scale research project in your class. When you write for readers other than yourself, you need to give special thought to how your ideas are best presented. You will need to bear this in mind as you work through this project.

Down the middle of each page you will find instructions explaining what to do. On either side are photographs of a class of students who tackled this survey, and examples of what they said and wrote. You will need to work with a partner or in a small group.

1
Discuss what your survey will be about.

We thought about what we'd do. We didn't think anybody else would decide to do 'Free Time', so we thought it'd be a good idea to find out what people did in their free time.

It could have been on anything really – about like what people do in the mornings before they go to school, but we decided to do it on hobbies instead – what people's favourite hobbies are and where they do them; like what teams they support and who their favourite players are; their football teams. . .

2
Talk to your teacher about your plans.

We wrote out this chart. . . well a questionnaire for people to fill in and then photocopied a lot of them and gave them one each to fill in. . .

Hobby Questionnaire

1. What are your favourite hobbies?
   Football
2. On what day(s) do you do them?
   Every day
3. If one of your favourite hobbies is football, who are your favourite team(s)/player(s)?
   Rangers, Spurs, Man. UTD, Oldham.
   Gary Lineker, Paul Gascoigne, Brian McLair and Paul Warhurst.
4. Why?
   Because they are brilliant
5. Do you play for any teams?
   Yes Reddish Vulcans and School
6. If one of your hobbies is an outdoor sport, would you play whatever the weather?
   Yes
7. Why?
   Because I like it
8. If your hobby includes going to some kind of sports ground, do you attend regularly?
   Every week (football match)

. . .They gave them back to us and we sorted through them and wrote it down on a piece of paper and did some graphs about them.

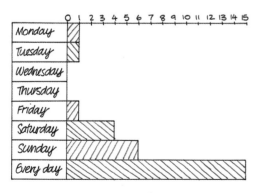

3

Discuss the kind of questions you want to ask. Make a list of them. Decide how you will ask them and how you will record people's answers.

4

Before you ask the questions to your class, talk about the various ways you might present the information. Jot down all the possible formats you could use and try to imagine how to make the results interesting to a variety of audiences such as your friends or parents.

5

Now ask your questions and record your results.

We wrote down the list of questions that we were going to ask them and then we decided whether to do a questionnaire or . . .but we interviewed them on the tape recorder. . .

			Total
Spurs	III		3
Man. Utd	IIIIIIIIIII		11
Oldham	II		2
Liverpool	II		2
Celtic	I		1
None	IIIIIIIII		9
None	IIIIIIIIIIIIII		14
Paul Stewart	I	14	1
Paul Ince	IIII	6	4
Paul Gascoigne	III	4	3
Bryan Robson	IIII	11	4
Mark Hughes	II	5	2
Gary Lineker	II	7	2
Neil Webb	I		1
Gary Pallister	I	9	1
Steve Bull	I	3	1
Ronnie Rosenthal	I	12	1
Nevil Southall	I	10	1
Earl Barrat	I	2	1
John Barnes	I	1	1
Andy Ritchie	I	10	1
Brian McClair	I	8	1
Paul Wadhurst	I	15	1

. . .and then when we'd finished asking everybody the questions we listened to it and wrote down all what we. . . what the answers were. . . and the results, really.

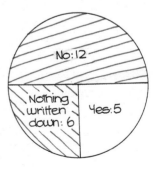

6

When you have gathered the information, discuss in pairs how it can best be presented on paper for each of the following purposes:

- so that you can remember the results easily.
- as interesting material for the rest of the class to look at.
- to influence a group of people who might not otherwise agree with your findings.

7

Choose one of the three options, and work on it together. Think about the various formats you discussed earlier. Think of your audience and the purpose of the writing. Decide how best to present your ideas and information.

8

Write a draft of your material. Consider its strengths and weaknesses. If you want to, show it to others in the class to get their advice. Write a final draft.

9

Each choose one of the two remaining options for presenting your material. Draft out a rough plan of how you intend to present the information. Discuss it with your partner. Write the final version, taking into account any advice you may have received.

Free Time

1. Do you have any hobbies?
2. Do you go to any discos/clubs etc?
3. Do you have a boyfriend/girlfriend?
4. Do you spend more time with your B. or G. friend or normal friends?
5. Do you go out every night?
6. Where do you go?
7. Do you do any homework before you go out?
8. How much free time do you get?
9. In your free time do you help around the house?
10. Is there anything else you do in your free time?

Lee:
Cycling
No!
No!

Not every night
Walking
Sometimes
A Lot
No!
No!

Lyndsey:
No!
Sometimes
Yes
Game
Yes (Not Mon.)
Park
No!
Not a lot
Yes
No!

Hobbies	Discos
Football	Yes
Listening to music	No
Football	Sometimes
Football	No
Football	No
Skateboarding	No
Cycling	No
Watching Videos	No
Animals	Yes
Sports	Sometimes
	Sometimes

Out every night
Yes: 10
No: 3
Sometimes: 5

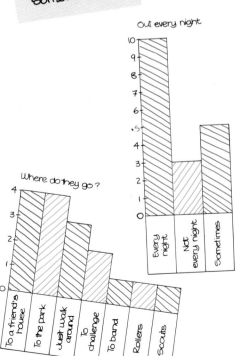

when we asked them if they had boyfriends or girlfriends we were a bit surprised because all the girls had boyfriends but none of the boys had girlfriends. . . then when we asked them about homework only three people did their homework so that was surprising because we thought that people'd say that they did it even if they didn't 'n' a lot of people get free time a lot of free time and hardly any people help around the house for their parents 'n' nobody does jobs for their parents apart from four people and nearly everybody goes out every night

10

The same information has been used to produce three different kinds of writing. What are the main differences between the three formats you have chosen? How does each of them achieve a different purpose?

11

Now you are going to present the material in a different way. You are going to tell the rest of the class what you have been doing. Think about how you will do this. You may want to use some of the charts you have prepared, to illustrate what you say. You may want to make some short notes to remind you of the main points.

12

How did your spoken version compare with the written versions you made earlier?

Are Children Lazy?

Some parents say that their children are lazy.
We have done interviews and proved most of them right.

Most people who are not lazy would not go straight out at night. They would do a few jobs for their parents and do their homework.

In 3AC only three people do homework and one person does sometimes.
Homework is important if you want a good education but people don't understand that, otherwise they would do their homework.

Parents do need help sometimes but most of them end up doing the work themselves.
Not many people help unless they are asked.
If parents are good enough to give their children free time then the children should be prepared to help their parents.

Diary of a wart

Friday 4th October

Susie's got the dreaded warts. They've sprouted on her thumb. I think
they look horrid and dirty. Wonder if it's because she sucks her thumb.
Hope I don't catch them. No one will hold hands with me, just when I've
made a start.

Saturday 5th October

She's becoming a real toady wart-hog. She's got them on her feet too. I
thought you got verrucas on your feet, but that turns out to be just another
name for warts on the feet which grow inwards because of the pressure.
She's busy painting her feet with stuff called salicylic acid from the
chemist. She says it kills off the warty skin and then you have to scrape it
off with a pumice stone. Don't much like having a bath after her – not
that I have one very often anyhow. At least now she's got something
other than her weight to worry about.

Sunday 6th October

Three of Susie's friends came to 'play'. Tea consisted of wart talk. Put
me right off my egg and toast. Her friend Kate said you had to get hold of
a piece of raw steak, rub it on the wart, and bury it. Trouble was when she
did it her dog kept digging it up and eating it. Her mum said to use
Dogameat next time, as it was cheaper, and anyhow her warts had spread.
Now she was trying her gran's recipe – wiping it with the juice of a
dandelion stalk, and putting the broken dandelion on to the thorn of a rose

116

bush. With luck, when it died her wart would fall off. If it didn't her gran's next best remedy was attending three funerals, and saying each time, as the funeral bells were ringing, 'Please take my warts with you.' Mum said that when she was young (a long time ago) you had to spit on your warty hands every morning. She tried it and it didn't work, but then she kept forgetting. Mary said Susie could try peeing on her hands, but I suggested the local swimming pool instead.

Monday 7th October

Worried. Something's growing on my knee. No one's hand has been there recently, but I'm spitting on it every hour, just in case. Keep missing but it helps clean my shoes.

Friday 11th October

Mum's taking Susie to someone called 'a chiropodist' tomorrow to have her verrucas fixed. Didn't explain to Mum about my knee but said I would come too, to keep them company.

Saturday 12th October

A chiropodist turns out to be a 'foot specialist' – smelly work if my feet are anything to go by. She said the spot on my knee wasn't a wart, just a pimple, and it would be better if I stopped spitting on it. She checked my feet, and gave me a lecture on how important it is to have well-fitting shoes. Otherwise you can get corns and callouses which are caused by rubbing from badly-fitting shoes. They are not something you catch, which is what I had thought.

When it came to Susie's feet (and I don't know how she could stand getting close to THEM), she got quite excited and started a new lecture

about how warts, whether on the hands or feet, ARE catching. They happen when wart viruses (and apparently there are several different kinds) get into cracks or cuts in the skin. As with my athletes' foot, swimming baths and changing rooms are common places to get the infections. They happen most in children aged twelve to sixteen, but some children NEVER get them, some get just the odd one, and some get lots and lots. No one knows why (seems to be a lot that people don't know about when it comes down to it).

Over half of the warts disappear in two years, even if you do nothing about them. Probably explains why all that digging meat into the ground, and going to funerals, SEEMS to work. If you use any of the medical treatments, like salicylic acid, then three-quarters will clear up in three months, which seems a bit better. For the ones that don't go away with this treatment, then burning, freezing or scraping away the dead skin often helps.

All this seemed to make Susie feel happier, though she had expected hers to go away overnight after she had tried the acid, and she didn't fancy the burning or freezing parts. The chiropodist said Susie can go swimming as long as she wears a plaster to cover her verrucas.

Sunday 13th October

Bits of Susie's dead skin on the bathroom floor this morning. Used downstairs toilet instead. Sam came round reeking of so much Brut that it was difficult to breathe. Told him that although in the natural world there are lovely smells, like flowers, it doesn't mean that they suit humans.

The truth

1 Look through the passage to find which parts of the diary are likely to provide you with accurate information about warts.
2 Make a note of the facts you find.
3 Present your findings as an information sheet for other pupils entitled 'The Truth about Warts'.

The myths

1 If those are the truths about warts, what are the myths? You will need to look carefully at the diary in order to sort these out.
2 Make a note of what you find.
3 Present your findings as an information sheet to accompany your previous one. You may call it 'The Wart Myths' or choose an alternative title of your own.

Presenting information

1 Are you happy with the way you have presented your two information sheets?
2 What would make them easier to understand?
3 What would make them more interesting to read?

Diary form

1 Do you think that the extracts you read came from an actual diary? Why or why not?
2 What advantages can you see for writing in diary form?
3 What do you think is the purpose of this diary?

You try

Now you try giving health advice in the form of a diary like the one you have been reading. Use the information given below.

'I have heard grown-ups say that watching a lot of TV will damage your eyes.'

This is just not true. If it were there would be a lot of adults who would damage their eyes before any of the children.

Like doing anything to excess, though, watching a lot of TV isn't a very good idea. In America it has been worked out now that by the age of three American children may spend 25-30 hours watching TV every week. While this may not cause any physical harm (except perhaps a sore behind from sitting) it is obviously a lot of time to fritter away. And, more important, if the programmes are rubbish then the young child may start to think along the same lines and not realize there is anything better.

Even the good programmes cannot compare to the excitement of real life or a well written adventure story. If you are spending seven hours a day in front of the telly you are clearly missing out on other things.

Another question is whether reading in poor light damages your eyes. As someone who first read all the James Bond books by the light of a torch under the bedclothes at my boarding school I have always had an interest in this.

The answer is that it does not damage the eyes. It may make them ache, though. When you read in poor light you tend to hold the book close. This is especially true when you are under the bedclothes with a torch!

Now when you look at a book close-up the eye has to do two important things: first it has to focus. It does not do this like a camera. Muscles actually change the shape of the lens. For near

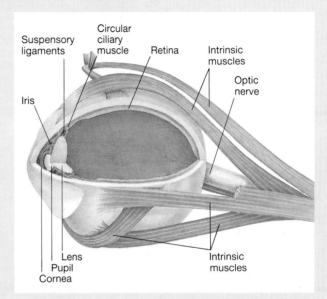

work these ciliary muscles contract. Ligaments holding the eye are relaxed. And the lens, which has an elastic cover, gets fatter.

Second, as you have two eyes, muscles outside the eye have to line them up so that they both look at the same part of your book. (If they did not you would notice double vision.)

So here are two sets of muscles working hard, perhaps in the glare of torchlight. It is not surprising that you may notice your eyes aching. And while no permanent damage is being done, any weakness that the eye already has may show up, perhaps as a squint.

All in all it's best to read in good light with the book at a comfortable distance.

Ideally as you read this, the book should be about 45 centimetres away.

Dr Peter Rowan

Soap story

'Strewth it's crook in the arvo'

Yesterday's TV *by Miles Smile*

Ardent fans of Australian soaps will need no translation of the headline above, but those of you who have had the sense to avoid the imports from Oz might need a little help: My goodness! It's not very good in the afternoon.

Indeed, it is not very good at any time of day, and the flood of Australian programmes is such that British television is in danger of being completely taken over by them. It might not be long before our screens are filled from morning to night with third rate series from Down Under. There are those who will welcome more revelations of the lives of everyday Sydney/Melbourne/Adelaide folk, but the time has surely arrived to call a halt.

The latest addition to the list of Antipodean atrocities is in the mould of its predecessors, and that is condemnation enough. BBC1 has introduced *Family Circle* to be shown three times a week from 6.30 p.m. to 7.00 p.m. But they need not have bothered. Within minutes of the start of the opening episode the well-tried pattern had emerged. Does someone really write this stuff, or is it spewed out by computer?

The family of the title are the Richardsons, and the hero is the blond, tanned eldest son, Craig (played, if that is the right word, by Bruce Druse), whose occupation appears to be surf-boarding. The heroine is Arlene (Sheila Wheeler), the daughter of Craig Richardson Senior's former business partner who is at present serving time in gaol for embezzlement from – you've guessed it – Craig Richardson Senior (Bruce Bushman). Arlene's occupation is fluttering her eyelashes at Craig Junior, and letting her lower jaw sag a lot. The resident gossip and laughing-stock is Mrs Wurzle (Sheila Singlet), who is related to the Richardsons in some complicated way which I lacked the interest to untangle. Need I go on?

It is only a matter of time before someone has a near-fatal car accident, someone else is wrongly accused of a crime, and Mrs Wurzle's malicious tongue brings the family to breaking point. The predictability of the plot will be as mind-numbing as all those that have come before. And talking of numb minds, the cast of *Family Circle* carry on the national TV acting tradition of conveying as great a range of emotions as synchronized swimmers.

The Australians can produce decent films. Why is it, then, that their TV is so pathetic? It is a big country: surely there is a kangaroo out there somewhere who can write a reasonable script; there has to be a wallaby who can act; and there must be a koala who can build a set which does not tremble every time a door closes.

What do you think?

1 In the first paragraph there is a phrase which gives us a clue to the writer's opinion about these programmes. What is it?
2 In the second paragraph there is another phrase which does the same thing. What is that?
3 Which word in the second paragraph suggests that too many programmes are imported?
4 At the end of the article the writer lists a number of criticisms. What are they?
5 How do you feel about these criticisms?
6 Miles Smile seems to think that Australian soaps are awful. In what ways would you agree or disagree, and why?

A question of tone

An important part of Miles Smile's message is in the tone of his article.

1 Is the word 'revelations' in paragraph 2 meant to be taken seriously? Why does he use it?
2 What does he mean by the word 'stuff' in paragraph 3? Why does he use this word?
3 Why does he refer to animals in the last paragraph?
4 How would you describe the writer's tone in this article? What leads you to this conclusion?

Writing

1 Write a letter to the editor of the newspaper, agreeing or disagreeing with Miles Smile. You could refer to characters or events in particular programmes to support your argument.
2 Write a newspaper article in the 'Miles Smile style', criticizing a TV programme (or type of programme) that you particularly dislike.
3 Write a newspaper article, to appear on the same day as Miles Smile's article, but in another newspaper. You are a TV critic and have seen the first episode of *Family Circle*. You think it will be just as good as the other Australian soaps you have seen and enjoyed. Your report should be as full of praise as the other one is full of criticism.

(CRAIG is cleaning the car. Enter NEV and ARLENE)

NEV: G'day sport.

CRAIG: G'day, Nev.

NEV: We're having a barbie on the beach.

CRAIG: No kidding?

NEV: Yeah. You coming?

CRAIG: What, now? This arvo?

NEV: Yeah. Too true.

CRAIG: No worries! I'll be right with you.

(Exit CRAIG)

ARLENE: Now there's a stroke o' luck.

NEV: You like him, doncha?

ARLENE: W..e..ll.

NEV: C'mon, Arlene. You really like him, doncha?

ARLENE: Aw, give it a rest, Nev.

(Enter CRAIG)

CRAIG: Bruce is round the back, cleaning the pool.
             I'll ask him as well, shall I?

NEV: No, no, hang on.

CRAIG: Wotcha mean?

NEV: We..ll, no offence, mate. I know he's your brother an' all,
             but. . . Well, he's a real drongo.

CRAIG: What was that again?

NEV: Drongo, mate. Drongo! You heard me.

(CRAIG approaches NEV threateningly)

CRAIG: You bludger! Call Bruce a drongo, wouldja?

ARLENE: Ne. . .v! Cra. . .ig!

NEV: Stay outa this, Arlene. (He tries to push her aside)

ARLENE: No, I won't. I've a mind of my own, y'know. Craig's right,
             you are a bludger.

NEV: Whose side are you on, anyway?

ARLENE: I don't have to be on anyone's side. But there's no need to call
             Bruce a drongo.

NEV: But he is a drongo, fair dinkum. Even a dag like you knows that.

ARLENE: Aw, rack off, Nev. Go and barbie by yourself.

NEV: Right, if that's the way you want it.

(Exit NEV, glowering)

ARLENE: I'm really sorry 'bout Nev, Craig.

CRAIG: I can understand that, Arlene.

Acting the scene

The aim of this is to produce a good 'walked reading' of the scene. A walked reading is a performance in which the actors still use their scripts, but know the scene well enough to be able to move and act with confidence. It is best done in a group of four:

> Arlene
> Nev
> Craig
> Director

1 Cast the parts and decide who will be the director.
2 Read the scene through together.
3 Discuss how it should be staged and acted.
4 Rehearse the scene until you are satisfied that you can give a good performance of it.

Group discussion

Is there anything in the script that you think of as being 'typically Australian'? Look at:
● the names of the characters
● the settings
● the activities that are mentioned
● the words and phrases that are used.

Dialect and stereotypes

The script is, of course, a spoof – a parody of programmes like *Neighbours* and *Home and Away*. It uses what are considered to be 'typical' Australian names, situations and expressions.

1 Make a list of the 'typical' Australian expressions it uses. Can you think of other words and phrases that you consider to be 'typical Australian dialect'?
2 British and American soaps and other dramas also use such expressions. For example:
> Leave it out
> Gerrouta my face

What other examples can you think of and where do they come from?
3 How many of these expressions do you think are genuine dialect, and how many are invented or exaggerated for the purposes of TV entertainment?

Writing

1 Write another scene for *Family Circle*, following on from this one.
2 Write a completely different scene for the same characters.
3 Rewrite this scene in a dialect you know well. For example:
> Glasgow Family Circle
> Geordie Family Circle
> Rhondda Family Circle.

Aussie TV station at standstill

Channel 10, Sydney's largest TV station, ground to a halt shortly after 6.00 p.m. yesterday evening. The switchboards were jammed by viewers calling to protest at the 'death' of Marge Richardson in yesterday's episode of Channel 10's *Family Circle*.

Marge, played by Sheila Hamm, perished in a fire at her home. Before the credits for the programme had finished rolling, angry viewers were making their feelings known to the station's directors. Hundreds of calls were made in the first few minutes, and by the time the backlog of incoming messages had been cleared at just after 10.00 p.m. last night, it was estimated that over 5,000 calls had been received. A number of viewers arrived at the station to register their disapproval personally.

'It's unbelievable,' said a spokesman for Channel 10. 'We are still shell-shocked. About half the telephone calls were abusive, and were demanding the resignation of everybody from the managing director, through the scriptwriter to the teaboy. The other callers, mainly the later ones, were in different stages of distress. Some just broke down and were unable to say anything; others asked that messages of sympathy should be passed on to the family. A few were enquiring about funeral arrangements. We already have three wreaths in our offices which were delivered before half past seven.'

The producers of the programme would not comment on the response to last night's 'tragedy', but a production assistant is reported to have claimed that Marge's death was TV's best kept secret. The episode was taped more than six weeks ago, and attractive, 37-year-old Sheila Hamm has been in Hollywood for the past month rehearsing a mini-series for American TV.

Last night's 'death' episode of *Family Circle* will not be screened in this country until early next year.

Questions

General

1 Do you know of any similar instances where people have confused fiction and real life?
2 How is it that some people can become so involved with fictional characters?

Looking closely at the text

3 In which paragraph is the headline explained?
4 Where do we read more details of this explanation?
5 Why does the writer quote what someone has actually said when he/she could have summed it up in his/her own words?
6 What is the point of describing Sheila Hamm as '. . .attractive, 37-year-old. . .'?

Death threats to actor

Actor Bruce O'Bong who plays drunken headmaster Cobber Stiles in the Australian soap Family Circle, has received anonymous death threats at his luxury home on the outskirts of Sydney. Cobber Stiles was seen by millions of viewers to start the fire in which Marge Richardson perished.

Since then, Bruce claims, his life has been a misery.

Shop assistants have refused to serve him, and he has been abused and spat at in the streets.

'It's not very pleasant,' says Bruce, 'but at least I have the comfort of knowing that I've convinced the audience that Cobber is a bad guy. My brother, Bill (also an actor), had to put up with the same sort of thing when he ran over a dog in an episode

of *Vet Knows*. But the letters are something else again. This is serious. I'm really worried.'

It seems strange that in a country where real life murderers no longer face the death penalty, an on-screen manslaughter should generate enough emotion to lead to an actor being sentenced to death by at least one fanatical viewer.

More stories of the stars

Here are ideas for other newspaper or magazine stories. Change the names around if you wish – or make up headlines and stories of your own on a similar theme.

Sheila Wheeler – the stress of stardom

Druse threatens to quit

At home with Sheila Singlet

The secret life of Bruce O'Bong

Why Marge had to go

The interview

Laverne Archer is a Jamaican actress who lives and works in London. In this interview she talks about her work and about Jamaican accents and dialects. In order to follow what she is saying, you need to listen to the interview on the cassette.

Laverne Archer

At the time of the interview, Laverne was working with the black theatre group, Umoja.

126

Interviewer: When you were little did you always want to be an actress?

Laverne Archer: Always. I couldn't wait to come home from church in the days
to put on a performance for my mother 'cos she didn't go to church. So I would
get on top of the chair and started going at . . . like the minister and stuff like
that. I would go to the post-office and I would watch the woman and I would
come back and I would play the post-mistress and stuff like that. Coming from
a very small rural area in Jamaica.

Interviewer: So what sort of things did you use to act? Did you use to act anything?

L.A.: Mm. When I was very small I did a lot of poems for um competitions and
stuff like that – um – a friend of mine just came to my mother trying to find a
little girl – somebody to play a silly little country girl and he thought I would
play the part well. I got the part and from there I ended up here.

I came here in '87 to do a play 'Don't Blame the Postman' and it was so successful
they had me back here this. . . in '88 again and from there on I've just been offered
parts in West Indian plays although I'm dying to do something different because
sometimes I find it difficult to speak properly *(laughs)* not 'properly' 'cos I regard my
Jamaican language as proper language even though some people mightn't feel the same.
There's a lot of problems going on now – especially in Britain I notice. Jamaican parents
don't want their children to speak Jamaican dialect. I don't know why. It comes across
quite silly especially for the teenagers who are getting into the Jamaican thing and they
want to speak Jamaican. It sounds just so silly and – um – I think people should be proud
of their language. I mean it's basically English though, you know. Because what happened
is – um – the Jamaican, uh the English came to Jamaica, plantation owners and stuff like
that and that's where we got our language from.

Interviewer: Do you find you're usually picked for Jamaican roles though?

L.A.: Uh huh, uh huh, but the good thing about it, especially the one I'm doing
now, it's a multi-role thing and I play about six different people in

that show and some of it, some of the – the roles are high-class Jamaican roles, so I get to speak properly, I get to behave – you know? – not that I don't mind but I think Jamaica's been portrayed as just a rough, nobody knows anything . . . smooth. . . or anything like that. Most of the plays tend to be a bit like that.

Interviewer: If I asked you to, to talk posh, to talk the way that someone who was very posh in Jamaica would speak, what would you do? Go on, do a bit for me.

L.A.: It's quite Americanized in Jamaica, so what you'd get from um, say, this would be about the girl, the average bank-teller, 'cos I tell you they speak different irrespective of where they live. Oh you go in the bank and everybody starts 'Hello, good morning, can I help you please?' *(laughs)* I mean that's not Jamaican really.
The, um, the Jamaican who doesn't work because he's rich speaks like. . . well . . . um

Whereas the Jamaicans down in Kingston, those that sell, may go to America and they buy and sell stuff. I don't understand them myself sometimes. It's like:

That's if you don't want something and you are just asking the price to find out if you can buy it.

128

And then there's the, the rebels now. Now these are hard core people I tell you about. This is what they would call Yardies now. I don't know what is Yardies, but that would be the equivalent to them in Jamaica. They have a different talk. It's

They don't get a sentence straight. They want to say something like, 'Well, what I'd like to tell you is that I haven't got any money, so I don't think I'll be able to make it to the theatre tonight, but if you'll pay for me, I'll come.'

That is them you know, the roughnecks they call them.

Interviewer: How many different sorts of language are there? I mean that's just three or four you've given me there.

L.A.: There's a lot. Because just as Liverpool differs from London, you should hear St Elizabeth people speak as opposed to those in St Katherine. They are really pretty people down there, I tell you. I find, I find it very funny listening to them. It's like, um: 'I was going to come and see you last week but it was raining.'

I can't tell you where that particular Jamaican language derive from, but it's mostly spoken in St Elizabeth and West Molanies. A slight difference from that in St Elizabeth quite near. St Andrew drawls the talking.
They talk:

St Katherine people – well they talk almost like Kingston people. If they speak, that's why they get away so much with some singing - that I don't know what it is. Specially the new type. I mean I'm young but some what the young people are singing now I don't like it at all. And they get away with it because the language you know, it's so singsong that even though they can't sing it comes out fairly nice.

Interviewer: Now when you were a kid, did you have any sort of silly sayings or rhymes or things like that?

L.A.: Oh, what were they now? I know. You used to have 'to clean a slate' because there was one time in Jamaica when we wrote on slates. It's, I don't know what it's – I think it's made of lead you know, and you have this pencil and you write on it. To clean it off, you have to get something wet and wipe it off. And kids used to put their spittle in their hand clap their hands together like this and then they would do:

if your slate is broken. . . And

130

Interviewer: What about if you're trying to convince your mum that you're telling the truth? 'Honest Mum, I'm telling the truth.'

L.A.: Well you couldn't . . . this one I'm going to say now you couldn't tell your mum that because that's blaspheming to your mum. But you could tell your friends or you could say, 'Honest to God' if you're talking to your mother, or 'God know', and she might still give you a thump for that but . . . really kids used to put your finger, put your index finger on your tongue. . .

and you touch it
on your forehead. . .

and then you roll
your hand over
your head. . .

and you say, 'Thunder roll and broke my neck'. Now if you are not telling the truth, when it rains you are worried! You are fright, 'cos you're sure you are going to die! But if you know you are telling – but people – I mean the kids were so scared of that that they don't do it unless they are telling the truth.

Writing an article

You are going to write an article based on the interview and the pictures.

1 Choosing your approach

Begin by thinking about your first reactions to the interview. Try to remember what you found most interesting and important in it. Think about your first impressions of Laverne Archer. Write these down briefly. Then decide who you wish to write for. It could be people of your own age, or for your parents, or for a magazine which is read by a variety of different people. Finally think about what 'line' you will take when you write.
(For example, do you want to focus on the dialect question, or are you more interested in her career?)

2 Preparation

Go through the interview again and listen to the cassette. Make a note of those parts that are going to be useful to you. Study these in more detail and write down the information, ideas and quotations that you want to use.

3 Drafting

Now you should be ready to write a first draft. If necessary, as you write, go back to the text or the cassette to check or add to your notes.

4 Sharing and discussion

For this you need to work with at least one other person. Exchange your pieces of writing and explain to each other what your intended audience is. Read and discuss each other's work. Make suggestions about how the writing could be developed and extended.

5 Re-working

Now re-read your writing, remembering what your partner said. Decide how you want to change what you have written. Produce a second draft.

6 Editing for publication

Now decide how your writing should be illustrated and presented. Select two or three of the illustrations in the book and decide where they should be used in your article. Decide whether they need captions to explain them. Think about using sub-headings and other devices to make your article clearer.

7 Published version

Now produce your published version.

Dialect

Much of what Laverne Archer has to say is about the different ways in which people speak. In particular she picks out a number of different dialects and ways of speaking to be found in Jamaica. You will have noticed that where she mimics dialect, this section is not written down and only appears on the cassette.

1 Make a list of the different places/kinds of people she mentions and imitates.
2 Some of her examples are 'social dialects': they belong to people who come from a particular social group. Which are these?
3 The other dialects are regional dialects: they belong to the people of a particular area. Which places does she mention?
4 Which of the dialects she mimics did you find easiest to understand and why?
5 Which of them did you find hardest and why?
6 Choose one of the regional dialects she mimics. Try to write down *exactly* what she says. Then write a version in Standard English. What are the main differences between the dialect and the Standard English?

A question of uniform

Our public image is very important and it stands to reason we ought to reflect that image in our clothes, doesn't it? So they give us a smart uniform. It's all right by me.

If you don't have school uniform then the kids all compete with each other to see who can wear the fanciest clothes – and that costs a packet, I can tell you.

If they want to supply me with my working clothes, who am I to complain? I don't want to mess up my own clothes, do I?

Your clothes – that's how you express yourself. People are different from each other. I don't want to go around looking the same as everybody else.

The uniform gives you a sense of identity. It's something you can be proud of – when you go down the street wearing it people look at you and they know who you are. They know you're somebody.

I think people ought to be allowed to wear what they like when they like. Why should people be forced to dress up the same as everyone else?

Uniform helps to identify you – so people know who you are straight away.

What you need are clothes that are suitable for the job you're doing. Then you know that you can do it well and that your clothing won't cause problems while you're doing it.

133

Uniform in hospital

Staff Nurse: Well start at the top and weve weve got sister she
wears a navy blue dress um with a navy belt whi- and sisters
always in navy so if anyones seen in navy that is a sister on the
ward then weve got staff nurse who wears a lighter shade of blue
5   and also with a dark blue belt next is the student nurse who
wears a blue check dress student nurses always wear caps with
a stripe for each year theres one blue stripe round the hat for the
first year student two for the second year and three for the third
year student and thats how we distinguish at which um part of
10   their training theyre at then we have the nursing auxiliary who
wears a white dress with a brown belt er nobody other than the
students now wear hats at all thats been done away with recently

Interviewer: A question that a lot of um people at school will ask
is why do we have to wear uniform why should we wear uniform
15   at all now now can you say one or two things about why its
valuable for people working in hospital nurses particularly to
wear uniform

Staff Nurse: I suppose to distinguish between patients and staff
and also you put your uniform on when you arrive at work its
20   therefore worn only in the ward er to stop any infection being
brought in from outside really and youre supposed to put a clean
uniform every on every day for the same reason basically for
infection purposes to stop any cross infection

Interviewer: So lets have a look at some of the things you you
25   actually that actually are included in the uniform Ive got the list
of uniform here and it begins um by saying that er you have to
wear an identity badge whats the point of that

Staff Nurse: Thats basically just for patient purposes to know who
theyre speaking to er really thats all and if anyone who visits the
30   ward um relatives and that sort of thing and new new doctors so
that they know who theyre actually talking to

Interviewer: So its a practical thing would it be true to say that the
point about most of the uniform is that its practical

Staff Nurse: Yes I would think so yes

35 **Interviewer:** Can you give examples of that

Staff Nurse: Um well shoes lace up shoes preferably and flat shoes covered toes um for the safety of the nurse basically pushing beds around you can damage your toes or drop things on your toes and you get a lot of back problems with the lifting that we have to do and with heeled shoes that in itself can cause *40* problems with the back so thats a very important factor is the type of shoes you wear

Interviewer: Now you dont to go to the the other end as it were you dont wear caps at this hospital any more apart from student nurses why wha whats the point of that *45*

Staff Nurse: I think basically years ago they used to wear different types of caps which covered the hair it was for infection purposes but over the years theyve just become a decoration really and didnt have any use at all so there wasnt really any point in wearing them the students still wear them just for the to *50* be able to wear ones with the stripes on so that we know which year they are and which part of their training theyre at

Interviewer: What about jewellery

Staff Nurse: Yes they do say only studs for the ears and not wrist watches and ri engagement rings you should only wear a *55* wedding ring basically because of lifting purposes you can scratch patients if youve got wrist watches and and um engagement rings on as you you know put your hand underneath the patient to lift you can scratch the skin so thats the purpose of that really *60*

Interviewer: Why dont doctors wear uniform

Staff Nurse: Um they wear white coats um the house doctors who are on the wards more so than any of the other doctors um but consultants definitely they dont they dont wear wear a uniform but theyre not dealing with the patients at such close contact as *65* as what the nursing staff are so um I suppose they think well were not bringing in infection like that you know that we could theyre not spending as much time with them

Interviewer: How would you describe the attitude of most working nurses to the kind of uniform they have to wear *70*

Staff Nurse: The majority comply fairly well you do get the odd ones who like to do their own thing and dont think that its necessary to stick to all these rules but the majority are they do stick to it yes

School uniform?

Different schools have very different attitudes towards uniform. On these two pages are two sets of school regulations about how sixth formers should dress.

School 'A'

Although the matter of dress is a personal choice you should remember that freedom of choice places a measure of responsibility on you, and that you are expected to conform to the sort of standard which could be reasonably expected in an adult community. It is often the case that students who wish to emphasize their reaction against wearing school uniform go to extremes of informality, even to the extent of cultivating a deliberate shabbiness. There is nothing new in this. The practice of these 'differentiation rituals', as the sociologists call them, is probably as old as civilization, but it often results merely in the adoption of a different kind of uniform (e.g. patched or torn jeans). However, as far as the College is concerned the way you dress is your own affair provided that you do not contravene the requirements of Health and Safety (e.g. by going barefoot) or offend against decency. Your clothing should be clean and in a reasonable condition, without unnecessary patches, holes, or deliberate frayed hems. In some institutions, such as secretarial, medical or business schools, students are required as part of their training to dress to a standard suitable to the profession they expect to enter. It would be impossible to set a common standard for our students because they go to so many different courses and jobs, but you should try while in College to learn to suit your way of dressing to the standards of an adult working community. It is often the case that the people who select candidates for appointments or College places are adversely and sometimes unreasonably affected by untidiness or a form of dress inappropriate to the occasion. This is also true of the general public on whose goodwill the College depends. If you use a measure of good sense in the way you dress you will help yourself as well as the College, whose task is to promote the wellbeing and prospects of all its members.

School 'B'

Girls

Please aim to look businesslike with either the uniform of school blazer, regulation skirt, white blouse, school tie or sixth form tie or a plain navy or plain grey suit of wool/polyester mixture (useful for interviews). No extreme lengths are acceptable. Shirts worn with the suit must have a collar and may be plain white, blue, yellow, navy or grey. The optional addition of a plain grey or navy, sleeveless or long sleeved, V neck or crew neck slipover or sweater in fine knit wool may be worn but it should match the suit colour.

Normal skin colour or navy tights. No bare legs or ankle socks, nor legwarmers.

Navy or black shoes, no stilettos, no suede, no down at heel shoes nor heavy brogues.

Makeup should be invisible.

Jewellery must be discreet and limited daily to one item or a small pair of earrings.

Plain navy, mid calf length, wool mixture coat. A plain navy or grey fine wool mixture scarf may be worn with it. These guidelines are intended to help you. If it is too difficult for Sixth Formers to look businesslike we may have to help by extending the uniform regulations.

Boys

The purpose of these guidelines is to allow a greater individual variation within the general uniform regulations which aim to encourage tidiness and produce a good public image.

School blazer and badge with medium or darker plain grey worsted or terylene trousers or a lounge suit (under the general supervision of housemasters).

Any authorized School tie, including the Governors' tie, or county colours ties.

Plain white shirts (rather than plain grey) should be worn, and Sixth Formers may wear V-necked pullovers of a plain colour if they wish.

Socks should be plain and appropriately sober (not white or day-glow orange for example) and shoes black or brown 'leather' polishable.

Outer garment should be a plain navy coat or plain navy anorak.

A plain navy or grey fine wool mixture scarf may be worn with it.

All articles must be named.

The suit

SIR CYRIL SMITH, the Social and Liberal Democrat MP for Rochdale in Lancashire, was fitted out yesterday for the suit he will wear when he is knighted by the Queen at Buckingham Palace on 2 November.

Apart from his mother Eva, 84, who will accompany him to London in her wheelchair, no one will observe Sir Cyril's stately progress with more anxiety and pride than his tailor for 20 years, Giuseppe Petrillo.

Sir Cyril's suit is being crafted in Rochdale from Mr Petrillo's stocks of finest herring-bone worsted wool, conservative in colour but jaunty in style. Despite Sir Cyril's faint misgivings, Mr Petrillo believes a gentleman should grow old frivolously.

'This is the special one,' Mr Petrillo said yesterday. 'We make hand-made suits only from the best cloth but this is really top-class. If I work for just Mr Smith it takes about six days to make the jacket. Say another three for the trousers. I've made maybe 50 for him over 20 years but this is not the biggest. No, no, it's about average.

I remember when I started he weighed 26 to 27 stone, now he's nearly 29 stone.

'In a way I charge him more because the material for a normal suit is about three metres and for him it is about seven-and-a-half metres. It's a lot of difference in the price. For him I've got two tape measures tied together. He's a bit difficult you know but he's not a problem to me.

'The only problem is when he goes in the fitting room and sits down. You allow a little bit of expansion in the jacket for a gentleman. But when he sits down he expands so much it's unbelievable. He doesn't stand up all the time so when you go on TV or sit down in the House of Commons you have to see the suit fit properly round the shoulders. It would not look good for the Queen if the jacket is going up on his neck.'

Sir Cyril said his fears about getting down on one knee for the ceremony had been allayed. 'I have been assured that there will be no problem because there will be a stool with handles so I can haul myself up after being knighted. There will also be attendants on hand to help as well.'

Peter Dunn, The Independent

This unit contains a number of texts on the theme of uniform. They are all genuine except for the quotations on page 133, which are made up.
On this page there are questions and assignments to guide you through each item. Then at the end there is a broader research and writing activity on the theme as a whole.

A question of uniform

These invented quotations reflect some of the attitudes people have towards uniform.
Study them and look at the illustrations.

1 Could any of the quotations be linked with any of the pictures? If so, make a list of them and explain why you think so.
2 Look at the pictures you have not mentioned in your list. What do you think each of these people might think about uniform?

3 Now look at each of the quotations in turn. Give each one a score from 1-5:
   1 I disagree strongly
   2 I disagree
   3 I have no opinion
   4 I agree
   5 I agree strongly
4 Choose the statement you agree with most strongly and explain why.
5 Choose the statement you disagree with most strongly and explain why.

Uniform in hospital

Different uniforms

Use the text and the picture to work out exactly what is worn by each of the following:
● ward sister
● staff nurse
● student nurse
● nursing auxiliary
Do the words and pictures always agree?
If not, what are the differences?
Now write clear descriptions of the four uniforms.

Reasons

The staff nurse describes a number of different reasons for nurses' uniform and the advantages that it has. They are listed opposite.
1 Find the places where she mentions each one. Write the letter of the point and the line(s) on which it is mentioned.
2 Add any other reasons or advantages you can think of. Give each of these a letter starting with (l).

Some of these points are more important than others. Think about this and then write down the letters in the order you think shows their importance.
   a to distinguish between patients and staff
   b so that patients know your name
   c to protect your feet
   d so that patients' relatives know who you are
   e to avoid cross-infection
   f to stop you scratching patients when you lift them
   g so that doctors know your name
   h to show how much training student nurses have had
   i to stop you hurting your back
   j to show what level of staff you are
   k to avoid bringing infection into the ward

School uniform?

A General impression
Read both sets of regulations. Think about your general impression of each writer and the kind of school each set of regulations must come from. How would you sum up those impressions and your reasons for them?

B Which school?
Look at the illustrations. Which of the students would not be acceptable at School 'A' and why? Which would not be acceptable at School 'B' and why?

C School 'A'
1 What effect does the writer think each of these factors should have on students' dress?
   a) Health and safety
   b) Public opinion
   c) Type of course
   d) Going to interview
   e) Personal choice and attitude
2 In what order of importance would you place these five factors and why?

D School 'B'
1 Do you think the Girls' and the Boys' regulations were written by the same person or by two different people? Is there anything in the text to help you decide?
2 What impression do you think this school would like its sixth formers to give? What is your evidence?
3 Do you think it trusts its sixth formers? What evidence is there for this?
4 What do you understand by the sentence 'Make-up should be invisible'? What does it tell us about the writer?
5 These regulations contain a number of key words which reveal a lot about the writer and the school. An example is 'businesslike' in the first line. What does the repeated use of this word suggest to you?
6 What other key words are there and what do they suggest?

The suit

Headline
This article came from a newspaper. It had a different headline from the one printed here. How would you sum up the article and the headline? Try to think of two or three possible headlines that sum up the subject matter of the article. Choose the best and explain why you think it is suitable.

Discussion points
1 Why do you think people wear suits?
2 Is a suit a uniform?
3 Why do people dress up specially to meet the Queen?

General

A school uniform
There are reasons for and against school uniform. Either
a) Write about this topic and examine the reasons for and against; or
b) Design your own school uniform and explain why you have designed it that way.

Uniforms in life
1 Think about all the ideas and information contained in this unit.
2 Find out more about the subject by talking to people, keeping your eyes open and looking at books and magazines.
3 Write a short illustrated article on the theme of uniform and different people's attitudes to it.

Theme park

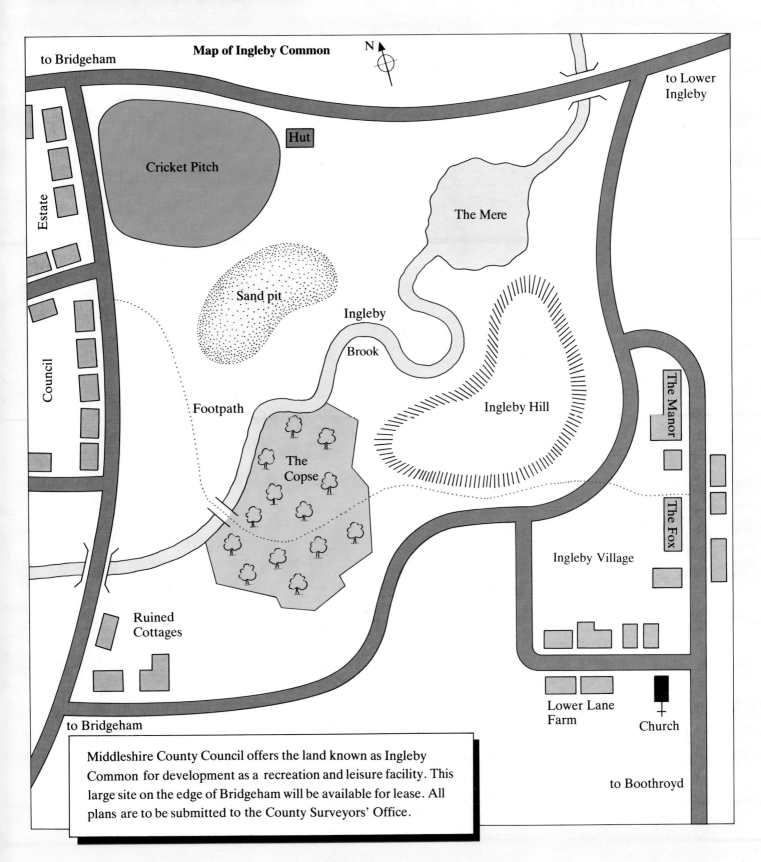

Map of Ingleby Common

N

to Bridgeham

to Lower Ingleby

Hut

Cricket Pitch

Estate

Council

The Mere

Sand pit

Ingleby
Brook

Footpath

Ingleby Hill

The Copse

The Manor

The Fox

Ingleby Village

Ruined Cottages

Lower Lane Farm

Church

to Bridgeham

to Boothroyd

Middleshire County Council offers the land known as Ingleby Common for development as a recreation and leisure facility. This large site on the edge of Bridgeham will be available for lease. All plans are to be submitted to the County Surveyors' Office.

Planning

Sleipnir Ride

Kraken Watersplash

Saxon Village
(Raids daily: 11.00, 1.00, 3.00, 5.00)

Tunnel of Freya

DARE YOU VISIT VALHALLA THEME PARK

What to do

1: Groups

You need to work in a 'development group' of three or four people. Each group has to design a theme park. The best idea will win the contract from the County Council.

2: Theme

Decide what your group's theme will be. You could have a brainstorming session – write down all the ideas you can think of in three minutes. (No discussion, no comments, just write them down.) Then discuss the ideas and choose the best. Remember that all the rides, refreshment areas and so on must reflect your theme.

3: Details

Now discuss the details and make a list of them. You could include:

rides
playgrounds
competitions
refreshments
shops
exhibitions

Valhalla Restaurant (The Food of the Gods)

Lucky Loki's Gaming Hall

Vikings' Fjord

Ferry

Norseman Harbour

Long Ship Lake

Erik Bloodaxe Bistro

Test your strength with Thor's Hammer

Draaken Railway

Asgarth Tower

The Grape and Pillage Meadhouse

Grendel Coaster

Dare you enter the Troll Caves?

Odin's Longhouse Indoor Play Area

Kingdom of the Dwarfs

R&D

FROM: Head of R & D
TO: R & D department

I want our park to be hairier, scarier, more exciting, more interesting, and more commercially successful than 'Valhalla' and 'Disneyland' put together - or some of us are going to wind up on permanent vacation, if you catch my drift. **Ideas soonest, please.**

Possible themes

Australian convicts
Back to the future
Cavemen
Under water world
Adventures on the lost planet
Merrie Englande

4: Plan

The next stage is to draw the plan of the theme park. Use the details on the County Council map. You'll probably have to do one or more rough versions before you do your final version. Label all the details, as the designers of the 'Valhalla' plan have done.

5: Submission

Now write a description of your submission, explaining it in more detail and saying why it is such a good idea.

6: Presentation

You have to present your ideas to the Chairperson of the County Council (your teacher) and the County Council members (the rest of the class). Decide how you will do this.

Taking sides

DEVELOPERS GET GO-AHEAD

The competition to develop Ingleby Common was decided last week. The successful firm of developers is expected to start construction work soon.

LOCAL TEXTILES FIRM CLOSES

Job losses

Bridgeham, already an unemployment blackspot, is to suffer further job losses as local textile firm, *Fashion Fabrics*, announced the closure of Ingleby Mill yesterday

Cricket ground under threat

Ingleby Cricket Club is threatened with closure, if plans go ahead to develop the site on which its ground stands. Club Secretary Major Teddie McEwan has reacted furiously to the news. 'Cricket has been played on the Common since 1876,' he told our reporter yesterday. 'W.G. Grace played here and ten years ago we were at Lords for the Village Cricket Final. If the ground is closed, it will be an act of desecration.'

PUBLIC INQUIRY CALLED

Local opposition to the development of a theme park at Ingleby Common has led to a Public Inquiry by the Department of the Environment. The Inquiry will be held

The Fox Inn

Fine Beers ... Good Food

Dear Gerald,

The local county set are kicking up a dickens of a rumpus over this theme park business and expect me to go along with them. But I'm not so sure myself - trade prospects could be very good indeed

Badger habitats threatened

The last badger sett known to exist in Middle-shire was threatened with destruction last week by plans to develop a theme park on Ingleby Common. The Common is also the home of a pair of goshawks. These rare birds have nested in The Copse, a small stretch of woodland, for the past three years.

Once again Christian values and tradition are under attack: this time by the proposed theme park at Ingleby. The Lord intended the Sabbath as a day of rest, but now our Holy Day will be made hideous with noise as pleasure-seekers troop to the Common while the church stands empty.

Because of complaints from local residents, a public inquiry is called to discuss whether the theme park should be built.
(At a public inquiry people are allowed to put their views forward.)
These groups will be represented at the inquiry:

   Townend Council Estate Residents
   The developers
   Ingleby Village Residents' Action Group
   The children of the area
   The local Environmental Group

What to do

1: Groups

Work in groups of 3-5. The developers will be the group which won the competition to design a theme park. Others represent one of the remaining groups in the list.

2: Reading

Before you begin to discuss the inquiry, read all the material on these two pages. Some of it will be useful to your group and some of it will be used by your opponents.

INGLEBY

2 mls E of Bridgeham, Middleshire
One of the most picturesque of Middleshire villages, Ingleby nestles

Chief among Ingleby's treasures, the Common (use of which was granted to local folk in the time of Edward II) is one of the unexpected beauty spots of Rural England. Especially important historically is Ingleby Hill, on whose summit stands the remains of an Iron Age hill fort, one of the best preserved in the country

From: Board of Directors

To: Planning Group

Who do these people think they are?
Your team had better

Arcue and Phibbs
Solicitors
Market Street
Bridgeham

The Manor
Ingleby

Dear Justin,   17 October

I simply cannot believe that there is nothing we can do to get this ghastly theme park stopped if the public inquiry decides against us. The area will be completely ruined -think of the noise - the traffic - coachloads of trippers - the mess - the litter - it's sheer wanton vandalism

---

Monday

110 Jubilee Buildings
Townend Crescent
Bridgeham

Dear Ma

Still no luck on the job front. Nothing in the Jobcentre, wrote off to six firms last week, not a sausage. Marge is a bit depressed about it all. Still, there's always the hope I can get something at this new theme park - if the snooty beggars in Ingleby don't mess it up.

Your loving son,

Sid

To the Leader of the Council
Dear Sir,
We, the kids off the Townend Estate wish to protest of your plans to take our Reccy off us. There is nowhere else for us to go. We don't want a theme park, we couldn't afford to get in anyway. We have wicked games of outlaws in the copse and a tarzan rope over the brook and the hill is great for tobog toob tarbogg sledding in winter. We have our own plans for the Common which are as

---

3: For or against?

Decide whether your group is for or against the theme park proposal.

4: Research

Look on these two pages for ideas and information that will be useful in building up your argument. Think of additional ideas of your own.

5: Preparing

Discuss how you will present your case. Organize your material and decide who will present which parts of it to the inquiry. Make sure you have clear notes to work from.

Public inquiry

At the public inquiry:

1 Each group has a spokesperson.
The spokesperson calls on different members of the group to explain different parts of their case, and sums up the group's argument at the end of the group's presentation.
2 Each group puts its case without being interrupted.
3 The Chairperson (your teacher) asks questions, if necessary, to make things clearer.
4 The spokesperson from each of the other groups is allowed to ask further questions.
5 Only one person speaks at a time.
6 At the end, the Chairperson sums up the arguments and decides who has 'won'. If the objectors have made the best case, then the theme park does not go ahead. If the developers and their supporters have made the best case, then it does go ahead.

Organization

Working in role

Remember that you are working in role. You are either one of the developers, or a person from the Ingleby area who is either for or against the theme park. Stay in role throughout the inquiry.

How people behave

Writing it up

After the inquiry has finished and the decision has been made, many different people have to write about it. How they report what has happened depends on:

Audience – who they are writing for

Purpose – what they want to achieve by writing

Format – how their words will be presented to the audience.

As you work on this page, remember these three factors.

J.S. And that was how the final decision went. Later I talked to the leader of the Ingleby Environmental Protection Group, Celia Green.

(Cue in Celia Green interview)

C.G. ... a great occasion for all those who believe in the countryside.

J.S. But not everybody agrees with that opinion. When I questioned Brigadier Humphrey de Vere ...

Local radio

... so the developers had to fight hard to explain why it was necessary to invade this peaceful corner of the English countryside. They were asked some hard questions about the impact on the environment and also on local social life. The village cricket team

Local paper

Inquiry chairperson

Public Inquiry into the Ingleby Common Theme Park Development Proposal

Those present:

Developers

Wonda**L**eisure **O**pportunities PLC

17th July 1991

Ingleby Common Project

I attended the Public Inquiry on behalf of the Development Team. I was accompanied by the following members of the team:

What to do

1 Think carefully about what happened at the inquiry.
2 Make a list of the different groups that were represented.
3 Against each one list the main points that were made by the speakers from that group.
3 Choose one of the four reports to write.
4 Think carefully about audience, purpose and format.
5 Write your report.

*L*ike a kind of different kind of story

This unit is about the different kinds of story you can read. . . and write. Pages 148 to 152 contain examples of story-writing from a variety of books. The suggestions about what to do are on pages 153 to 155.

The covers

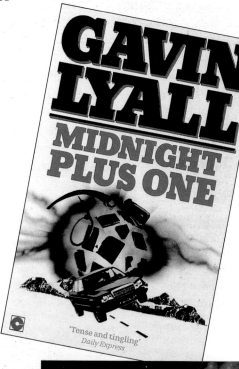

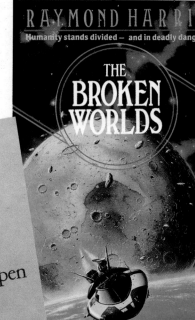

The blurbs

1

'The meeting begins at midnight tomorrow plus one minute. We have a little more than thirty-six hours.'

A former SOE operative, Cane knew the roads and border crossings of Europe like the back of his hand. All he and Lovell had to do was to drive an international financier from Brittany to Liechtenstein. Pretty routine stuff.

He should have known better. Merlin had hinted that there were those – the French police included – who were determined to prevent their passenger from completing the journey. No explanation. But when Cane found out why, he wasn't surprised that half the hit-men in Europe were after them.

The next thirty-six hours were going to be anything but routine.

2

Carol looked at the girl's chalk-white face, and her relief was clouded with doubt. Perhaps the terror wasn't over after all; perhaps it had only just begun . . .

She had appeared out of nowhere . . . in the middle of traffic, on a busy day, in front of Carol's car. A teenager with no past, no family – and no memories. Carol and Paul were instantly drawn to her, this girl they named Jane – she was the daughter they had never had. It was almost too good to be true.

Then the hauntings began – ghastly sounds in the dark of night; a bloody face in the mirror; a dim but persistent sense of fear . . . and the déjà vu.

Where had Jane come from? Was she just an orphan in need of love? Or was she hiding a more sinister purpose? Who was the girl behind the mask . . . ?

3

What do teddy bears talk about when they're by themselves? And what's life like for a teddy when his owner has grown up and his growl has worn out? This delightful and amusing picture book explores the private worlds and thoughts of Ted and Teddy, teddy bears to capture every bear lover's imagination.

4

MARS – centre of the fractured universe, planet of immortal warlords and cloned warriors – fallen now to outsystem invaders.
PARMENIO – grimy haven for the desperate and the decadent.
LOEI – world of towering peaks, rife with intrigue and danger, rumoured hiding place of the fabled fleet of Old Earth.
YNENGA – desert home of the bird-like Tu'u, with shifting sands that hide ancient secrets.
VIHARN – a world divided, where cloud dwellers turn traitor, and landsmen hold the key to survival.
Through these kaleidoscopic worlds stumbles a reluctant messenger, Attanio Hwin, and he carries a warning: disaster threatens from beyond the stars . . .
The Broken Worlds must unite – or die!

5

A MAGNIFICENT EPIC OF IMMENSE SCOPE SET AGAINST A HISTORY OF SEVEN THOUSAND YEARS OF THE STRUGGLES OF GODS AND KINGS AND MEN – OF STRANGE LANDS AND EVENTS – OF FATE AND A PROPHECY THAT MUST BE FULFILLED!

It had all begun with the theft of the Orb that had so long protected the West from the evil God Torak. Before that, Garion had been a simple farm boy. Afterward, he discovered that his aunt was really the Sorceress Polgara and his grandfather was Belgarath, the Eternal Man. Then, on the long quest to recover the Orb, Garion found to his dismay that he, too, was a sorcerer.

Now, at last, the Orb was regained and the quest was nearing its end. Of course, the questors still had to escape from this crumbling enemy fortress and flee across a desert filled with Murgo soldiers searching for them, while Grolim Hierarchs strove to destroy them with dark magic. Then, somehow, they must manage to be in Riva with the Orb by Erastide. After that, however, Garion was sure that his part in these great events would be finished.

But the Prophecy still held future surprises for Garion – and for the little princess Ce'Nedra!

6

'Without warning, someone stepped out of a dream . . .'

Holiday jobs aren't supposed to be hard work. But Allie finds that 'helping out' in a seaside restaurant really means near slave labour in a dingy cafe – and being expected to look after two fractious toddlers.

She's on the brink of leaving – but then she meets Paul and his funny friend, Beef, and suddenly the summer is transformed. For Allie falls instantly for blond, blue-eyed, hunky Paul and, to her astonishment, he seems to feel the same way about her . . .

A punchy, modern novel from the author of *Stick* and *Just How Far?*

The writing

A

'What kind of a bear are you?' asked Ted.

'I'm an Idle Bear.'

'But don't you have a name like me?'

'Yes, but my name is Teddy. All bears like us are called Teddy.'

Ted thought for a while, then said, 'Well, Teddy, I have been Ted forever – at least fifty years, I think.'

'Me too,' said Teddy, 'at least that long.'

We could be related, thought Ted and Teddy together.

'We are related!' announced Ted, pretending he had known for ages.

'How can you tell, Ted?' challenged Teddy, 'How do you know?'

'Oh, I just know. Everybody has relations, I think, especially where I come from,' said Ted beginning to wish it wasn't so.

'Where do you come from, Ted?'

'From an idea,' said Ted definitely.

'But ideas are not real, they are only made-up,' said Teddy. 'You have to come from somewhere real to have realitives.'

'Not realitives, relatives!' said Ted trying to hide his confusion.

B

It was dark and my mouth was full of slime and there was a distant rattle like a large-tooth file dragged across my raw brain. And deep inside, pain. The sort of pain you don't want to disturb, that you want to leave sleeping – but you know it won't sleep. But *you* can sleep. Just lie there. And sleep. And maybe die.

The idea jerked me awake. If I was dying, at least it meant I wasn't dead yet. I spat and tried to roll up on to my side – and that hurt. A flare of pain like a lighted fuse ran clear through me.

I kept very still and it died to a dull red ache around my stomach and a heavy feeling in my legs. *God, not a stomach wound, not a bullet in the guts and living on milk the rest of my life. And you can bribe a doctor into patching up a bullet scrape and calling it a road accident, but a hole in the belly is going to get reported. . .*

At least I was thinking like Caneton again. And come to that, why should a stomach wound paralyse my legs? I screwed my head around and saw the dead man lying across the back of my knees.

I looked carefully around. I was lying at the bottom of the pillbox steps, and just ahead of me was the body of the man I'd shot. The Rolls' lights were out.

The rattle started again, and this time it didn't feel distant. Bullets crunched and screamed at the lip of the trench and somebody dropped into it with a heavy splash. I groped in the mud for the Mauser, found it, then Harvey said: 'Cane – are you alive?'

C   There was time only for a fleeting glimpse of the great Martian veilship before they docked. The Parmenite was amazed by its apparent delicacy. It had no external shell: instead its various components were exposed to the vacuum. Command modules, habitation cylinders, shuttle hangars, and Cluj-pulse drives were all arranged in a roughly conical pattern. A lacy network of struts and passage tubes strung them all together, and a refractive haze surrounded the whole with a subtle aura – apparently the Darabundit field. Overall it called to mind the skeleton of some leviathan of the void.

'Not like the old adventure cubes, is it?' Fsau of Myint jived, in oddly accented Ptok.

'Not a bit,' Attanio replied. 'So insubstantial!'

The alien's face held a peculiar expression. 'Yes, my friend, it can be that.'

Docking was imperceptible. They stepped out into a vast echoing hold, as chilly as Attanio had imagined space would be. He didn't have time to puzzle over the presence of gravity. Immediately the whole crew jumped into an umbilical and became weightless again, propelled along on a jet of air.

Sringlë took his hand and guided him gently. 'Welcome aboard *Samuindorogo*, love. You're about to have your first audience with the captain.'

'*Samuindorogo*? Is that supposed to mean something?'

'Cold Master,' she replied. Attanio wondered what those words implied for his future.

D   There, in the rain, was Paul, a coat round his shoulders, his hair dripping. And parked at the kerbside was his new car. It was too gloomy, too distorted by the rainfall for me to see clearly, but a pale hand waved to me from the passenger seat, and a pale remembered smile flipped my heart over. Beef. The shadow of that smile was enough. I felt certain, now, of where I was, and what I wanted.

Paul pushed past me into the cafe, flung his jacket on to a chair, and shook his head to clear the raindrops.

'So?' he asked, turning to me. 'Decided to play silly buggers, did you? Let me stand around in the Mariners, waiting for you, last night? I felt a total div! And it's the second time, too. There was Saturday night as well. What's wrong with you, Alison? You like showing people up or something? Gives you a buzz, does it?'

'Sorry about last night. . .' I stammered.

'So am I. Really. Anyway, it's too late now. You missed the going-away party. I've just come to collect my stock. Up here, is it?' he asked, storming through the cafe to the kitchen and the stairs.

'Just a minute!' I shouted, running after him.

E Ctuchik was dead – and more than dead – and the earth itself heaved and groaned in the aftershock of his destruction. Garion and the others fled down through the dim galleries that honeycombed the swaying basalt pinnacle, with the rocks grinding and cracking about them and fragments shattering away from the ceilings and raining down on them in the darkness. Even as he ran, Garion's mind jerked and veered, his thoughts tumbling over each other chaotically, stunned out of all coherence by the enormity of what had just happened. Flight was a desperate need, and he fled without thought or even awareness, his running steps as mechanical as his heartbeat.

His ears seemed full of a swelling, exultant song that rang and soared in the vaults of his mind, erasing thought and filling him with stupefied wonder. Through all his confusion, however, he was sharply conscious of the trusting touch of the small hand he held in his. The little boy they had found in Ctuchik's grim turret ran beside him with the Orb of Aldur clasped tightly to his little chest. Garion knew that it was the Orb that filled his mind with song. It had whispered to him as they had mounted the steps of the turret, and its song had soared as he had entered the room where it had lain. It was the song of the Orb that obliterated all thought – more than shock or the thunderous detonation that had destroyed Ctuchik and tumbled Belgarath across the floor like a rag doll or the deep sullen boom of the earthquake that had followed.

F Paul couldn't decide what the poltergeist intended to accomplish by its impressive displays of power. He didn't know whether or not he had anything to fear from it. Was it trying to delay him, trying to keep him here until it was too late for him to help Carol? Or perhaps it was urging him on, trying its best to convince him that he must go to the cabin immediately.

Still holding the suitcase in one hand, he approached the bedroom door that had been flung shut by the unseen presence. As he reached for the knob, the door began to rattle in its frame – gently at first, then fiercely.

Thunk. . . thunk. . . thunk. . . THUNK!

He jerked his hand back, unsure what he ought to do.

THUNK!!

The sound of the ax was coming from the door now, not from overhead, as it had been. Although the solid-core, raised-panel, fir door was a formidable barrier rather than just a flimsy Masonite model, it shook violently and then cracked down the middle as if it were constructed of balsa wood.

Paul backed away from it.

Another crack appeared, parallel to the first, and chips of wood flew into the room.

The covers

When we are choosing books in a bookshop or in a library, our first impressions come from the cover. Look carefully at these six covers and see what information each one gives you about the book. (To make things a little more difficult we have blanked words on some of them.)

1 What impression do you get of each book from its cover?
2 How would you describe the type of book each one is?
3 What is it about each cover that has given you these ideas? (The picture? The title? The lettering? The design?)
4 Which of the books do you think you might like to read and why?
5 Which of them do you think you would probably not like to read and why?

The blurbs

The 'blurb' is the information that the publisher provides – usually on the back of the book – to let you know what kind of book it is and, very roughly, what it is about.

1 What impression do you get of each book from its blurb?
2 How would you describe the type of book each one is?
3 What is it in each blurb that has given you these ideas? (For example, can you pick out particular words or phrases that tell you straight away what kind of book is being described?)
4 As you have probably realized by now, these blurbs belong to the same books as the covers on page 148. Which one goes with which – and how do you know?

The writing

The six extracts on pages 150 to 152 come from the same books as the covers and the blurbs. The covers and blurbs told us what the publishers thought the books were like – and how they wanted to sell them. The extracts show the kind of writing each author thought was suitable for the kind of book he or she was writing. Read each one carefully and then collect as much information as you can about the kind of book it comes from. It will probably help if you make up a chart like this:

Title	Blurb	Extract	Kind of book	Typical names	Examples of typical writing
Rendezvous on Sirius	7	G	Science fiction	Grozxvcmann	...entering the orbit of the mothership through a deep asteroid belt...

Genre

It is quite easy to identify what kind of book the examples we have quoted come from. This is because each book belongs to a definite type, or genre. Not all books are easy to categorize like this. (And some, of course, belong to more than one – for example the historical romance.) Sometimes writers can get a lot of fun out of deliberately mixing genres. Which genres have been mixed in this short extract?

Once upon a time on a tiny little planet far out in the solar system lived a strange creature called Ertgraophi. Ertgraophi was a very very wicked android and it wanted to have all the solar system to itself. . .

Writing in a genre

Now it is your turn to try your hand at writing in a genre. It could be one of those which you have been studying in this unit, or a different one that you enjoy reading yourself.

Planning

1 Begin by deciding which genre you would like to work on. It should be one you know something about, but it need not be one that you have written in before.
2 Find examples of your chosen genre in the school or local library, or at home. Study them to make sure that you have a good idea of the writers' style and approach.
3 Work out the basic plot of your story. Remember that you are only writing a short story, not a five-hundred-page blockbuster, so don't try to cram too much in. Write out a short outline of the plot.
4 Think carefully about how your story will start. It is important to catch the reader's interest as quickly as possible. Have a look at the books you found that illustrate your chosen genre – see how they do it.

①

Thriller - 'Revenge is sweet'

1. Car driven down country lane is attacked by hidden gunman. Driver is killed. Gunman escapes on motorbike.
2. Funeral of dead man. He was a British secret service agent. His killer has been murdering other top American and British agents. His twin brother, also an agent (codename Jekyll), is present.
3. Secret service HQ: Jekyll is taunted by another agent, Hottgang, who doesn't realize his brother is dead. Head of Secret Service tells Jekyll he can't go after his brother's killer, but Jekyll insists. Hottgang decides to help him.
4. Jekyll and Hottgang on the trail of gunman - they find a motorbike just like the one used by the killer.
5. Gunman comes out, sees Jekyll, and thinks it's his dead twin brother. Gunman escapes on motorbike.
6. Car chase. Gunman heading for spot where brother was killed. Jekyll and Hottgang get there first.

②

Some people didn't know about Hyde's death. One man called Hottgang thought everything was a huge joke and never took anything seriously.
'Hey, Jekyll, where's Hyde today?' Hottgang shouted down the corridor. Jekyll turned and walked menacingly towards him.
'If you're trying to be funny I'll rip your head off!'
'Hey, what's wrong man?'
'Hyde is dead, and so will you be if you don't let up with your cheap wisecracks.'
'I had no idea. But that's a hell of a heavy thing to lay on a guy first thing in the morning!'
'Well, I'm going after the murdering swine who's been killing the American agents as well.'
'How do you know?'
'He used the same technique of killing. An automatic machine gun, he obviously springs up out of nowhere and kills his victims. The tracks of the bike match those of the other tracks we've found near the killings. The bike we're looking for is a Harley Davidson, but modified. It has the same body, but the engine has been replaced and is much more powerful. I've got a list of places where this creep is known to hang out. The bike has been mostly seen in the area of the Heavy Rock Café.'

Building

1 Now it is time to start writing your story. Let the ideas flow and concentrate on making the story interesting for the reader. From time to time check that you are following the rough plot outline you made earlier.
2 When you have finished this first draft, read it through and think about the genre you are writing in. Have you followed the approach and style of the books you looked at when you were planning? Can you develop your own story so that it is a better example of the genre?
3 Now work with a partner. Show them what you have written and ask them to comment:
   ● does it make sense?
   ● can they understand it all?
   ● can they suggest improvements?
Remember that at this stage you are concentrating on the story and the way it is written, not the spelling and punctuation.
4 Now go back to your story and rewrite those parts of it that you think need improving.

Editing

When you have finished building and developing your story, it is time to edit it.

1 Read it through and think about the way in which you have written your sentences. Look for:
  - sentences that seem confusing and can be made clearer
  - too much repetition of the same word, that can be avoided by the use of different words
  - use of vague words like 'nice' or 'kind of', which can be replaced by sharper, more precise words.
2 Check for spelling mistakes. If in doubt, use a dictionary, or ask.
3 Look at your punctuation. Imagine yourself as the reader of the story: does the punctuation help the reader as much as it could? If in doubt look at the punctuation section at the back of this book.

3

Not everyone knew
~~Some people didn't know~~ about Hyde's death. Holtgang was one of them; but then, maybe that didn't ~~One man called~~ Holtgang ~~thought everything was a huge joke~~ make much difference. ~~and~~ never took anything seriously.

'Hey, Jekyll, where's Hyde today?' Holtgang shouted down the corridor. Jekyll turned and walked menacingly towards him.

'If you're trying to be funny I'll rip your head off!'

'Hey, what's wrong ~~man~~?'

'Hyde is dead, and so will you be if you don't let up with your cheap wisecracks.'

'I had no idea'. ~~But that's a hell of a heavy thing to lay on a guy first thing in the morning.~~

'Well, I'm going after the murdering swine who killed him. ~~who's been killing~~ the American agents ~~as well~~! The same man who killed

'How do you know?'

'He used the same technique of killing. An automatic machine gun, ~~he obviously~~ — the same weapon. ~~springs up out of nowhere and kills his victims~~. And the tracks of the bike match ~~those of the other~~ other tracks we've found near the killings. The bike we're looking for is a Harley Davidson, but modified: ~~It has~~ the same body, with a more powerful but ~~the~~ engine. ~~has been replaced and is much more powerful~~. I've got a list of places where this creep is known to hang out. The bike has been ~~mostly~~ seen in the area of the Heavy Rock Café.'

4

Not everyone knew about Hyde's death. Holtgang was one of them; but then, maybe that didn't make much difference. Holtgang never took anything seriously.

'Hey, Jekyll, where's Hyde today?' Holtgang shouted down the corridor. Jekyll turned and walked menacingly towards him.

'If you're trying to be funny I'll rip your head off!'

'Hey, what's wrong?'

'Hyde is dead, and so will you be if you don't let up with your cheap wisecracks.'

'I had no idea.'

'Well, I'm going after the murdering swine who killed him. The same man who killed the American agents.'

'How do you know?'

'He used the same technique of killing. An automatic machine gun — the same weapon. And the tracks of the bike match the tracks we've found near the other killings. The bike we're looking for is a Harley Davidson, but modified: the same body, but with a more powerful engine. I've got a list of places where this creep is known to hang out. The bike has been seen mostly in the area of the Heavy Rock Café.'

Publishing

'Publishing' simply means making your work 'public' – so that other people can read and enjoy it.

1 Think about the format you are going to use:
  - the size of page you will write the story up on
  - the way in which the pages will be held together
  - how it will be written or printed (could you use a word processor, or typewriter?)
  - whether it will have illustrations, and if so, how these will be linked to the words.
2 Now write or word process your story.
3 When it is written, design a cover for it. (Remember how the covers on page 148 gave the reader an idea of the subject matter and the style of the stories.)
4 Finally, write a back cover blurb, similar to those on page 149.

The tree of death

Geoffrey Chaucer lived in the 14th century. He worked as a diplomat and civil servant for King Richard II. He was also a poet. His most famous poem is *The Canterbury Tales*.

Bifil that in that seson on a day,
In Southwerk at the Tabard as I lay
Redy to wenden on my pilgrimage
To Caunterbury with ful devout corage...

Every year pilgrims travelled to the shrine of St Thomas Becket in Canterbury cathedral. They went partly as tourists – to have a good time and see an interesting place – but also because they believed that this journey would be good for them as Christians. It was a sign of their devotion to their faith.

Chaucer sets his poem on such a pilgrimage. In order to pass the time as they travel, the pilgrims agree that each of them will tell a story. Each story reflects the interests and character of the person who is telling it.

At night was come into that hostelrie
Wel nine and twenty in a compaignie,
Of sondry folk, by aventure yfalle
In felaweshipe, and pilgrimes were they alle,
That toward Caunterbury wolden ride.

The Pardoner

Chaucer begins *The Canterbury Tales* by describing each of the pilgrims. Among them was a **Pardoner**.

At this time people believed that if you committed sins you would go to hell when you died. If you confessed and received absolution from the priest then you would not go to hell, but as well as confessing, you also had to do a *penance*: say a number of prayers, or perform some other duty as a punishment. Then the Church introduced written *indulgences* or 'pardons'. In return for a payment of money or goods, you could be let off the penance or punishment. It was these pardons that the Pardoner sold. He also had a collection of *holy relics*, which he claimed would produce miracles, and which people were allowed to touch if they paid him a small fee. In both these ways he was able to profit out of the simple faith of ignorant people.

This pardoner hadde heer as yelow as wex,
But smothe it heeng as dooth a strike of flex;
By ounces henge his lokkes that he hadde,
And therwith he his shuldres overspradde;
But thinne it lay, by colpons oon and oon.

A voys he hadde as smal as hath a goot.
No berd hadde he, ne nevere sholde have;
As smothe it was as it were late shave.

Chaucer's language

Chaucer lived in a society where educated people could speak three languages: Latin, French, and English. He chose to write *The Canterbury Tales* in English. As you can see, it was not exactly the language we speak today. But it is possible to work out what he meant.

1 Some words are exactly the same in modern English. If you look at the extracts on these pages you can find several examples.
2 Some words are similar, but spelled slightly differently:
   seson   redy   Caunterbury
   See if you can find other examples.
3 Other words are either very different from their modern English, or no longer exist at all:
   colpons = strips, thin bunches
   Go through the extracts and make a list of the words that you cannot recognize or work out.

4 At times the order of the words is different from what you would expect. Sometimes this is because it was different anyway in Chaucer's time, at other times it is because he has changed the order so that the rhyme and the rhythm of his poem will work:
'pilgrimes were they alle'
(= they were all pilgrims)
In this case, you have to study the sentence carefully and try to work out what a modern word order would be. A good way to start is to discover what the subject of the sentence is and then work from that.

Word list

clepeth	call
erst er prime rong of any belle	before 6 o'clock in the morning
felawe	friend
habitacioun	home (habitation)
haunteden	gave themselves up to
hine	labourer
mo	more
page	servant
pardee	indeed
privee	secret
riotoures	revellers
sleen	slay, kill
sleeth	kills
smoot. . . atwo	struck. . . into two pieces
stirte	jumped
swich peril	so dangerous
trowe	think
whilom	once upon a time

Telling the story

Use the pictures and the word list to help you work out what happened. Try to find answers to these questions:

1 What kind of people are the three young men in the story?
2 What reason are they given to explain why so many people are dying?
3 What do you think the real reason is?
4 What do the three of them set out to do?

Acting the story

This part of the story consists of a conversation. Think about the questions that follow and then act out a modern version of it:

1 Where does it take place?
2 Who are the characters?
3 What are the most important parts of the conversation?
4 How does it begin and end?

Word list

artow	are you (= art thou)
but mighte this gold be caried	if only this gold could be carried
carl	fellow
cherl	villain
fil	fell
florin	a coin worth a third of a pound in Chaucer's time
han	have
in heigh felicitee	very happy
lafte	left
leef	keen
livestow	do you live
ne dooth	do not do
of gold ycoined	made of gold
ook	oak
partest	go away
thilke	that
with sory grace	bad luck to you
wol	will
wolde	would

Telling the story

Work out the story as you did before. Think about these questions:

1 Why does the young man mistrust the old man?
2 How does the old man explain himself?
3 What do you think of his explanation?
4 What do you think of the behaviour of the young men when they find the gold?

Acting the story

As before, you can act out a modern version of this story. This part divides into two sections:

1 In the tavern.
2 In the wood.

Think about these points:

a) How could you transfer these scenes to a modern setting?
b) How might the old man be dressed?
c) How would they speak to him?

161

He filled with wyn his grete botels thre. To his felawes again repaireth he.

Now lat us sitte and drinke, and make us merie, And afterward we wol his body berie.

And with that word it happed him, par cas, To take the botel ther the poison was, And drank, and yaf his felawe drinke also, For which anon they storven bothe two.

Word list

accorded been	agreed
anon	at once
bitwixen	between
departed	shared
doon	do
natheless	nevertheless
oon	one
par cas	by chance
pothecarie	apothecary, chemist
repaireth	returned
rive	stab
shrewes	rogues
shul	shall
storven	died
thridde	third
thurgh	through
tweye	two
woost	know
woot	knows
yaf	gave
yhent	seized

Writing a story

You can use the material in this unit as the starting point for your own version of the story. You can set it in the Middle Ages, or in modern times. Think about these points:

1 What are the characters of the three young men? (Are they all much the same, or are they different from each other?)
2 What are their names?
3 What is their way of life?
4 Who is the old man? (And if it is a modern story, what does he look like and how does he speak?)
5 Who is telling the story? What is the storyteller's attitude to the characters in it?
6 If you are telling a modern version of the story, you need to think about where the different scenes take place.

163

RADIO REMPTON

Radio Rempton

Rempton is a small town in the north of England, about 180 miles from London. The local radio station, Radio Rempton, has recently opened. To mark its opening, the station has decided upon a novel experiment. For a whole day all the programmes will be made by teenagers, for teenagers. The idea is to make them feel the station has something to offer, and to get them to tune in right from the start. The experiment is open to everyone; all you have to do is to produce a 'demo' tape which shows how well you can make some sample programmes.

The programmes

The formats for the programmes have been decided already as they will form part of regular series on the new station. Details of the programmes required have been circulated to all schools, and these appear in the following pages. They include:

Teenage Helpline
Problems are aired, and advice is given, by a panel of experts on teenage issues.

Sports Desk
brings up to date news on all the local sporting personalities.

Dramatime
Write an episode of *The Odd Jobbers,* about a bunch of teen-age 'workers'.

Ask the Experts
You ask the questions, they come up with the answers.

Down Your Way
You don't need to go far to find interesting people with unusual things to say about themselves.

Kids' Korner
Write a story for young listeners about *The Dins*

What you have to do

You will be working in small groups to produce a tape containing your sample of programmes. You will need to know how to do the following things:

1 Use a tape recorder, both to record and to edit your programmes.
2 Take part in interviews, role-playing either the interviewer, or the person being interviewed.

3 Research any information you need for your programmes.
4 Write scripts.
5 Talk clearly and effectively, so that your audience can understand you easily.

The first thing you have to do, though, is to find out what these programmes are all about, and which your group intends to choose.

Teenage Helpline

Teenage Helpline is a programme aimed at offering advice to both teenagers and their parents. Adolescence is often a time of stress. Some of the problems it brings may seem trivial, others are much more difficult to talk about or solve. Whatever the problem, sensible, sympathetic advice is needed. The programme offers the help of a panel of experts, doctors, social workers, and youth workers. It invites teenagers or their parents to contact the panel, either by letter, or on the phone-in. A selection from the post bag appears below.

Dear Helpline,
I think I know about a serious problem, but I don't know what I should do. My best friend came to school the other day and I saw she was covered in bruises. She made up some excuse, but I think someone has been hitting her. What can I do, who should I tell?
Bernie

Dear Helpline,
I feel terrible. Last week my thirteen year old son was caught stealing sweets from a local newsagents. There were a group of his friends doing it too, all daring each other. But the shopkeeper called in the police, to make an example of them, he said. I feel my son has really let me down, but he doesn't seem to take it seriously at all. He seems to think it's all a big joke, and has made him 'look big' in the eyes of his friends at school. How can I make him realise that what he did was wrong, and that I'm afraid he'll get into more serious trouble later on?
Distressed Mum

Dear Helpline,
What can I do about two girls at school who are making my life a misery? It's hard to explain. You see when I am with them one at a time, they are fine and are good friends. But when I'm with both of them, they pick on me, and make personal remarks. I'm smaller than them you see. It's as much the way they say it as what they say. They seem to be worse when there are boys around for some reason. I've tried going round with other people but that didn't work. They just went on about 'not being good enough for her'. What else can I do?
Katie

Dear Helpline,
This may seem a silly problem, but I just can't stand PE or games at school. It's not the actual lessons I mind, I just don't like having to have a shower afterwards. Whenever I refuse, the teacher gets really mad and says I have to because its healthier, and a school rule. But I think it's really embarrassing. We should be allowed to have some privacy or else choose whether to have a shower or not. The teachers do as much running as we do (sometimes!) but they don't bother with showers. Or else they've got their own shower in their own room. It's just not fair. What can I do?
Embarrassed

Dear Helpline,
My parents are being real stick in the muds. A local disco has started running 'Teenage Nites' from 7pm 'til 10pm on Thursday evenings. All my friends go, but I can't because this disco is in a 'rough part of town' (they say). It is a 'real' nightclub I admit that, but these nights are special and are only for 13 to 16 year olds. Help me convince them I can go.
Left out

Dear Helpline,
My parents just don't seem to get on together lately. They row all the time and say horrible things to each other. I just can't stand it and am thinking of running away. I couldn't bear it if they got divorced, but when I try to find out what the matter is they won't talk about it. It's my life too — how can I make them see what they're doing to me?
Francis

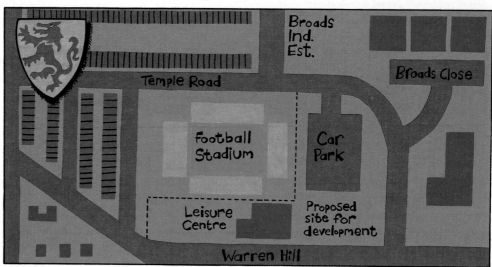

Terry Burke
'Players need to be disciplined and work hard.'

Danny Williams
'A woman for manager? What do you think we've already got?'

Marilyn Hill
Stepping up into the big time?

Town in turmoil

The hot story of the moment concerns Rempton Town Football Club. The 2nd division team are haunted by relegation fears and have financial problems off the pitch. They currently lie bottom of the table, and haven't won for seventeen matches. Plans to make some desperately needed cash by selling land attached to the stadium to a supermarket chain have caused uproar.

The development would involve demolishing several rows of terraced houses on Temple Road and Warren Hill. The club owns these houses, and rents them to tenants, some of whom have lived there for more than twenty years. On the site, there would be built a Leisure Centre, a Supermarket and Car Park.

The tenants are reluctant to move, though the club has offered them compensation. They have complained about threatening letters and damage to the houses. The money is needed to bring the ground up to legal standards, and to buy new players. Even the proposed Leisure Centre has caused arguments about what types of sports should be catered for. A suggested dry ski-slope has been much criticized as an irrelevant luxury.

Fans have called for the sacking of the manager, Terry Burke. The players' morale is said to be rock bottom following his decision to fine heavily several of his stars who went out drinking the night before a key game.

Several players have asked for transfers, and say that they have no confidence in the manager. These include the club captain Danny Williams. After a story in *The Sun*, he faces a charge of bringing the game into disrepute.

The Board have told Mr Burke that they support him one hundred per cent. He claims that the present problems stem from their decision to sell U21 international Paul Fick to Manchester United. Hints that a woman will be the next manager have been denied. Marilyn Hill, the manager of non-league Fordwell Town, has so far made no comment about the rumours.

This could be a real scoop for the station if you can get these people talking! Try to arrange interviews with them all, and the Chairman, Ivor Ball. Find some fans and get their views. Don't forget the tenants. How about a studio discussion? Could be hot stuff!

Dramatime

Dramatime is a weekly drama series aimed at a teenage audience. The episodes being planned at the moment are about a group of teenagers who try to make some money by doing odd jobs, as a kind of business. They call themselves the 'Odd Jobbers'. Some of the jobs they do are very odd indeed! No job is too small, and no job is too difficult. From repairing cars to hunting ghosts, minding babies, and running a homework service, they'll tackle anything. And whatever they do, it's bound to go wrong. The truth is that they're not very good at anything. Full of ideas and good intentions, but rather lacking in the practical skills to carry out the job successfully. As a result, they find themselves being pursued by a vengeful army of adults, parents, clients, teachers, even the odd policeman. Each episode finds them in ever more difficult situations from which they only manage to escape by the skin of their teeth.

Ideas for the main characters have been suggested. These appear below. The characters can be changed if better ideas are put forward, but there must be clear differences between each of them. Each character should be clearly presented in the episode so that listeners get to know them quickly.

As well as the 'Odd Jobbers' themselves, a number of adult characters will appear in each episode. These also need to be invented.

Mickey is the good-natured member of the group. Full of fun, and willing to do anything. But likely to put his foot in it! He acts first and thinks later. He thinks that things will turn out all right in the end. Usually they don't.

Sumitra is the quiet one in the group. She stays in the background, and is put upon by the others who never listen to the good advice she offers. She usually has to sort out the mess the others have made, if she can. . .

Tessa spends most of her time and energy making herself look attractive. She objects to doing anything which may spoil her clothes, her hair, her nails. . . Totally unreliable, gives up easily, and often forgets to turn up at all.

Paula is the ideas person in the group. She is always making great plans, but is no use at all at carrying them out. Always noisy, she'll argue at the drop of a hat. Blames others when things go wrong, and abandons ship.

Justin has a gloomy sense of humour. He is convinced that everything is bound to go wrong, even on the rare occasions when things are going well. Always pleased to tell the others 'I told you so'. Fancies Paula. . .

An opening storyline has been thought up. The Headteacher is going on a skiing holiday with the school and needs someone to look after his garden while he's away. He's very proud of his plants, and wins prizes for his onions. Paula offers the services of the group, and the Head naturally declines. She persuades the others it will be good publicity to do the job anyway, to show what they can do. Off goes the Head, leaving his onions unprotected. . .

Just ordinary people? Don't you believe it! Everyone has a story to tell or something to say. Find out more about the people who live in Rempton when you go. . .

Down Your Way

Down Your Way is a human interest programme which aims to introduce a wide variety of people to the radio audience. The researchers for the programme have provided a list of people who may have interesting things to say about themselves. Your job is to choose which of these local 'celebrities' to interview. What questions could you ask them to get them talking on their favourite topic? What would listeners like to find out about these people? Their jobs, their hobbies, their ambitions, their lives – get them talking!

Marjorie Rose runs the 'True Heart' dating agency. A former model, actress and dancer, she now tries to help lonely people find romance. But why has 'Mr Right' not appeared in her own life yet. . .?

Gill Sharp is a private investigator. Not as glamorous a life as it seems since much of her time is spent debt collecting, or tracing lost pets. But there have been some cases when her life has been on the line. . .

Norman (Jessie) James may work in a bank by day, but at the weekend he's working out how to rob them! As members of the local Wild West Society, he and his wife Sylvia like to re-live the good old days way out west. . .

No place for a woman, they said. Aboard a spacecraft with five men. But Molly Higgs is looking forward to the greatest adventure of her life. A Doctor of Physics, she has been chosen to go on the next Shuttle launch. . .

Tom Crop is known to children as 'the wild man of the woods'. He lives alone in a small wooden hut in a local copse. Rat-catcher, poacher, and expert on animals, what is it that has made him choose this style of life. . .?

Guldip is certain he is going to make his fortune one day. One of his many inventions is sure to work. Until then he'll continue to experiment in his garage. Perhaps the hover shoes weren't such a good idea, but this one. . .

What's it like to put your head in a lion's mouth, be shot from a cannon, perform on a trapeze, eat fire, escape from chains, or keep performing fleas? Ask Cyril. He's done all these things in his time in the circus. . .

Percy Forsyth was born in 1900. He has fought in two world wars, and lived through all the historic events of the century. He has seen many changes during the course of his lifetime. What stands out in his memory. . .?

168

Want to find out how to do something?
Need some information or advice?
No matter how strange or unusual, why don't you. . .

ASK the Experts

Ask the Experts is a programme which gives people advice and information about anything and everything. Each week, listeners write or phone the programme with their requests. A sample from the postbag is given below, but you may be asked how to pan for gold, keep ferrets, buy a horse, decorate a bedroom, go scuba diving or make it rain! You need to find out the answers by doing some research, and then give clear instructions and information. Here are the questions. . . now over to the experts for some answers.

Dear Experts,
I'm looking for an unusual pet, something a bit out of the ordinary. Everyone's got a cat or a dog or a goldfish. I want something a bit special. How can I persuade my mum to let me keep a tarantula, or a piranha? What do I keep it in? How do I feed and look after it? Can I take it for walks (joke - sorry!)? Any other suggestions?
Suzy

Hail Dungeon Masters!
I've recently started to play Dungeons and Dragons. My friends all seem to know much more about it than me. They even cast their own models. Can you give me a quick guide so I can surprise them?

Mary

Dear Experts,
How did the Egyptians make their Mummies? Why did they bury people in this way, and is it true the bodies are still actually OK? Sorry if this seems a bit grisly. I'm just curious.
Gary

Dear Experts,
I have decided not to eat meat any more and to become vegetarian. Trouble is, my mum doesn't know what to cook, and the rest of the family say it's all 'rabbit food'. Any ideas please?
Tony

Dear Know-alls,
My dad has these odd ideas sometimes. The latest is a holiday on a canal barge. Where is the best place to start from, and what's the furthest we can travel? Are they easy to sail?
Yours damply,
Kate

Dear Experts,
I have this terrible problem. I just can't get to sleep at night. I've tried all the usual things like counting sheep but they don't work. Can you help me out?

Yours tiredly
Lisa

Kids korner

Kids' Korner is a programme intended for 3 to 6 year olds. Each day there is a short story about a group of characters called 'The Dins'. Each of these has a name and personality which is suggested by the way they speak, or sound. You have to invent the next story in the series.

Dozey Den spends most of his waking hours asleep! He can't be trusted to do anything properly without falling asleep in the middle of it. He's not very bright when he's awake either! Yawns and snores a lot.

There's always romance in the air whenever Kirstie Kiss is around. She is forever falling in love, and spends much of her time sighing deeply. Her kisses have to be heard to be believed!

If you're feeling down in the dumps, then Laurie Laughs is the bloke to cheer you up. He's always acting the fool and telling jokes. (This sometimes gets on people's nerves!) He laughs like water in a plughole (only louder).

Poor Trisha Tishoo is just the opposite. She is always gloomy, and convinced that she's got horrible diseases. She spends a lot of the time telling people how poorly she feels, and just complaining about things. Sneezes a lot.

'Spuds' Slurp is forever hungry, always eating, yet stays as thin as a rake. Wherever he is he munches, crunches or makes terrible slurping sounds (especially in cinemas). He has absolutely no manners at all!

Winnie Whisper enjoys only one thing – gossip. She is incredibly nosey, and spends all her time finding out things about the rest of the Dins – things which cause trouble when she passes them on. She always speaks in a low, sinister whisper. . .

There's no missing Carol Trill. She's a large woman with a large voice. She loves to sing, and practises nearly all day long, opera mostly. She talks loudly too. A very bossy lady, she drives her neighbours mad. . .

. . .especially Roger Roar. Roger is so easy to upset he'd fight with his toenail clippings! He will argue with anyone about anything at any time. Underneath that aggressive exterior there's an aggressive interior. Watch out!

170

Presentation

Setting out letters

There are traditions about the way in which letters are written and set out on the page. They concern these parts of the letter:

The writer's address

Even if you know someone quite well, you still write your address at the beginning of the letter. Normally it goes in the top right hand corner, like this:

> 26, Burrington Lane,
> Herdridge,
>   Devon PL3 6GT

or like this:

> 26, Burrington Lane,
> Herdridge,
> Devon PL3 6GT.

The address of the person you are writing to

If you are writing a letter to a business, government department, or some other large organization, you normally put the name and/or title of the person you are writing to, their department, and the address of the firm.
The name and department are important because letters are often opened by someone else who then throws the envelope away. If you miss them out, your letter may not get to the right person.
It is not necessary to do this when you are writing an informal letter.

The date

In a formal letter this is usually placed after, or level with, the end of the address of the person you are writing to. It is written in full:

> 23rd July 1991

In an informal letter it comes after your own address and need not be written in full:

> Tuesday 3rd March   Tuesday

How the letter opens

This depends on how well you know the person you are writing to. For example:

> Dear Sir,   Dear Madam,   Dear Editor,
>
> Dear Ms Spencer,   Dear Mr Grant,

How the letter closes

This depends on how well you know the person you are writing to (and how you opened it). For example:

> Yours faithfully,   Yours sincerely,
> F.G. Harmer   F.G. Harmer
>
> Yours sincerely,   Best wishes,
> Frank Harmer   Frank
>
> Love,
> Frankie

It is normal to use 'Yours faithfully' in a letter that begins 'Dear Sir' or 'Dear Madam'.

Hartley Grantham & Wilcox
Merrow Chambers
High Street
Furle
Glos
GL56 9BX

Mrs H. Knowlesby,
17, Babberton Crescent,
Furle,
Glos,
GL56 7MC.

12th August 1988

Dear Madam,
It has been brought to our notice by our client, Mr Curtis, that he has been caused a lot of
trouble by the activities of your three-year-old son Timothy. He says that several times

17 Babberton Crescent,
Furle,
Glos.
Wednesday

Dear Marge,
A terrible thing happened yesterday. I discovered that young Timothy has

I really don't know what to do for the best. Of course as usual Dave
isn't a lot of help. He just says it's all my fault and in any
case what else can you expect from an old idiot like Curtis.
I think I'll have to go and say sorry and all that but I don't
see how I can make up for it. Any ideas?
All the best,
Hilary

and that unless you take action to prevent this happening again, he will be forced to take
further steps against you. I need hardly add that this would be not only very embarrassing
for all concerned, but also expensive both for you and for him. May I suggest that you meet
with Mr Curtis at your earliest convenience to resolve this matter.

Yours faithfully,

H. J. Hartley

H.J. Hartley

Punctuation

Capital letters

Capital letters are used for these purposes:

1 As the first letter of a sentence.

> Have a nice day.

2 For the personal pronoun 'I'.

> Last week I went to the zoo.

3 At the beginning of a new piece of direct speech. (See page 178.)

> At last he said, 'We won!'

4 For the first letter of proper nouns.

> People's names: Deidre Blackadder
> Places: Brentwood
> Titles of books, plays, films, TV programmes:
> > The Oxford English Programme
> Days of the week: Wednesday
> Months of the year: January
> Planets and stars: Jupiter

5 For the first letters of titles of people and organizations.

> Lady Windermere
> Foreign Minister
> Royal Society for the Protection of Birds

6 For initials in people's names.

> W. Shakespeare

7 For initial letters used in abbreviations.

> JP
> IBA
> NSPCC

Full stops, question marks, and exclamation marks

Normal sentences must end with one of these three marks. . ? !

Statements normally end with a **full stop**.

> It is easy when you know how.

A **question** normally ends with a **question mark**.

> Do you understand what I mean?

Exclamation marks are used to mark an **exclamation**, or a **forceful statement**.

> If only you would listen to what I am saying!

> **Warning!**
> If you use too many exclamation marks, readers will get very tired of them.

Abbreviations

If a word is shortened, or abbreviated, then you usually put a full stop after it.

> **M.K.**Thomas
> 4.5 kilometres **N.**
> **Ill.** (Illinois)
> **Col.** (Colonel)

There are a number of exceptions to this:

1 Abbreviations made up only of capital letters do not need full stops.

> **ANC**   **OUP**   **TUC**

2 Abbreviations that make up words (acronyms) do not need full stops.

> **ASH** (Action on Smoking and Health)
> **COSIRA** (COuncil for Small Industries in Rural Areas)

3 These abbreviations do not need full stops:

> **Mr Mrs Ms M** (Monsieur) **Mme** (Madame)
> **Mlle** (Mademoiselle) **Dr St Revd**
> **p** (= penny or pence)

Commas

Commas are an important way in which we can make our writing easier to read. These are the main ways in which commas are used:

① In lists

If a sentence contains a list then it makes it much easier to sort out what is in the list, if we use commas:

> In English there are several different punctuation marks, including full stops, apostrophes, commas and inverted commas.

This still applies if the items in the list are each quite long:

> He had an interesting collection of old toys: a Victorian doll's house, an early wooden rocking horse, several china dolls and a collection of lead soldiers.

Lists like this usually have 'and' before the last item. Some people say that you should never put a comma before this, but it depends. Sometimes you must put a comma before the 'and'. If you don't, it looks very odd:

> They had a very big menu for their school dinners: spaghetti, stew, salad, fried fish and fresh fruit.

② Putting things in brackets

Sometimes when writing a sentence we want to put in something that doesn't belong to the main part of the sentence:

> The heavy snowfall in Switzerland the first of the winter for many ski resorts has caused serious problems on many roads.

'The first of the winter for many ski resorts' doesn't have to be there. The sentence would make sense without it:

> The heavy snowfall in Switzerland has caused serious problems on many roads.

but 'the first of the winter for many ski resorts' adds useful information. You could put it in brackets:

> The heavy snowfall in Switzerland **(the first of the winter for many ski resorts)** has caused serious problems on many roads.

or you could use dashes:

> The heavy snowfall in Switzerland **– the first of the winter for many ski resorts –** has caused serious problems on many roads.

or you could use commas instead of brackets:

The heavy snowfall in Switzerland, **the first of the winter for many ski resorts,** has caused serious problems on many roads.

Words used in this way are said to be **in parentheses**.

3 To mark off the main sections of a sentence

When I got up, I noticed that it had been raining all night, so I went outside to make sure that everything was all right.

Colons

Colons are used to introduce a list, a saying, or a statement:

You know, I found the most extraordinary collection of things in his jacket pockets: two penknives, some used chewing gum, a five pound note, half a false moustache, and the key to his father's filing cabinet.

When they were near the top of the mountain, their leader turned and addressed them: 'Listen to me, all of you. What we are going to do now is very dangerous.'

There is only one rule on board this ship: don't rock the boat.

Semi-colons

A semi-colon is used between two clauses in a sentence. It makes a stronger pause in the sentence than a comma, but not as strong as a full stop. It is often used to separate two or more equal parts in a sentence:

Soccer is a game for gentlemen played by ruffians; rugger is a game for ruffians played by gentlemen.

It was a pitiful scene: some huddled together for warmth; some tried desperately to escape; others stood stunned and motionless.

177

Writing down speech

There are two ways in which you can write down the words that someone says:

1 script

2 direct speech

Script is normally used for plays. Direct speech is most commonly used in stories.

Script

1 The names of the speakers are put in capital letters, on the left hand side of the page.

2 The words spoken are written, without any special punctuation, a little way to the right. The speeches should all start at the same point in the line.

3 Information about an individual character who is speaking is put in the speech. It is put in brackets and underlined.

4 Information about other things that happen, including sounds and actions, is given a line to itself. It is put in brackets and underlined.

(Iris door opens and **HAL** enters. Before he is in room, **LOISE** speaks.)

LOISE: It's the big game show tonight, Hal.

HAL: And don't I know it. Everyone is talking about it and the vacuum tubes were packed solid.

LOISE: Everyone wants to get home early to be sure they don't miss it. What are you having for dinner?

HAL: (After a pause, while he thinks about this) Make mine a chicken salad with plenty of garlic salt. I'll have pineapple for dessert.

(**LOISE** goes to computer and programmes it. She presses out the code for the cookery index and then orders the meal.)

LOISE: I'm going to have a curry. Central Kitchens are getting better at making curry.

Direct speech

1 Each piece of speech is enclosed between double or single inverted commas. In books single inverted commas are normally used. In school pupils are often taught to use double inverted commas.

2 Every new picce of speech must begin with a capital letter, even if it is not the first word in the sentence.

3 Each piece of speech must end with a full stop or an exclamation mark or a question mark before the concluding inverted commas. . .

4 . . . unless the sentence is going to continue, when it ends with a comma. This also comes before the concluding inverted commas.

5 When a piece of speech comes in the middle of a sentence it must have a comma (or sometimes a colon) just before the opening inverted commas.

6 For each new speaker you start a new line and indent.

7 When something happens, or there is a sound or you want to describe how someone felt, you just write it as part of the story.

The iris door opened and before he could even get through to the lounge Loise was talking to him. 'It's the big game show tonight, Hal.'

'And don't I know it,' he replied. 'Everyone is talking about it and the vacuum tubes were packed solid.'

'Everyone wants to get home early to be sure they don't miss it,' Loise said. 'What are you having for dinner?'

He thought about that, then said, 'Make mine a chicken salad with plenty of garlic salt. I'll have pineapple for dessert.'

Loise programmed the computer, pressed out the code for the cookery index and then ordered the meal. 'I'm going to have a curry,' she said. 'Central Kitchens are getting better at making curry.'

Apostrophes

Apostrophes are used for two purposes:

1   To show possession (that something belongs to somebody).

2   To show omission (that something has been missed out).

Possession

1   Normally you add **'s**.

> That is the dog**'s** basket, not the cat**'s**.
> That is Maria**'s** book.

2   When the word is a plural ending in **-s**, we just add **'**.

> That is the gir**ls'** tennis ball.

Notice that these words do not have an apostrophe:

> hers   ours   yours   theirs   whose

When '**its**' means 'of it', you should not put an apostrophe.

Omission

When we are writing informally, or writing speech, we often use shortened forms. In these cases, the apostrophe shows where the letters have been missed out.

he is	→	heis	→	he's
they are	→	theyare	→	they're
I do not	→	I donot	→	I don't
it is	→	itis	→	it's

180

Spelling

Ways to better spelling

Write it down and try it out

Spellings are patterns and our brains are good at remembering patterns. If you aren't sure which of two or three spellings is right, try writing them all out on a piece of paper – which of them looks right?

Look for patterns

English spelling isn't chaotic. Three-quarters of all words are spelled according to a regular pattern. As you are reading and writing, try to be aware of the patterns of letters we use to spell particular sounds.

Learn the rules for changes

Many words have to be changed according to how they are used in a sentence. We have to add bits onto the end of them:

-s/es	one boss . . . several boss**es**
	I pass . . . she pass**es**
-ed	She taps . . . I tapp**ed**
	he rakes . . . I rak**ed**
-ing	I skated . . . they are skat**ing**
	I tip . . . we are tipp**ing**

If you learn the rules you will avoid a lot of the mistakes. These rules are explained on page 182.

Keep a spelling book

Either get a special notebook, or use the back of an exercise book. Write down the words you find difficult, so that you can look them up easily.

Use a dictionary

If you think you know how the word starts, look it up in a dictionary. If you aren't sure how it starts, try different versions out on paper first and look them up in the dictionary to find out which one is right.

Look for word families

Words go in families:

This family consists of four words. In all of them 'author' is spelled the same.
-ity -ize -ization are spelled in the same way as they are in other words (modernize, modernity, modernization, for example). If you look out for families like this, you will find spelling gets easier.

This is especially helpful with words that are linked like this, but pronounced differently:

| sign**ed** | sign**ing** | sign**al** |
| sign**ature** | sign**atory** | |

Use words

Never be put off from using a new word just because you are not sure how to spell it.

Read books

Read regularly. Reading will not make everyone a perfect speller, but it is difficult to be a really good speller if you never read anything at all.

How words are made up

If you know how words are constructed, it can help you to spell more accurately, and also to work out the meaning of new words.

Words can consist of up to three parts:

Prefix	Stem	Suffix
in	complete	ly

Stem

All words have a stem.
Many words consist only of a stem:

look	paper

Suffix

There are two types of suffix.

Fitting the sentence
The commonest, which we use almost every time we speak or write, are suffixes which are added to a word so that it fits into the sentence:

When I saw her she was look**ing** through the papers on her desk.

Common examples
Nouns can add **-s** to make a plural.
(Or sometimes they change in other ways.)
See page 184.

Verbs can add **-s** to change subject:

they wal**k**   she walk**s**

Verbs can add **-ed** and **-ing** to change tense:

we walk   we walk**ed**   we are walk**ing**

Adjectives can add **-er** and **-est** for comparison:

I am tall   she is tall**er**   he is tall**est**

Making new words
Other suffixes are used to make new words. These are some of the commonest:

-ly makes an adjective into an adverb:

sad**ly**, happi**ly**.

-ment makes a noun out of a verb:

excite**ment**, manage**ment**.

-ity makes a noun out of an adjective:

rapid**ity**, regular**ity**.

-ation makes a noun out of a verb:

explor**ation**, organiz**ation**.

-ness makes a noun out of an adjective:

happi**ness**, kind**ness**.

-ist makes a noun into another noun (which can also sometimes be used as an adjective):

violin**ist**, social**ist**.

Prefixes

A prefix is the part of a word that comes at the beginning, before the main part or stem:

un + happy	→	unhappy
super + man	→	superman

If you know the commonest prefixes and what they mean, it can help you to work out the meaning of a new or unknown word.

Prefix	Meaning	Examples
ante-	before	antedate
anti-	against	anti-apartheid
arch-	big, chief	archbishop
auto-	self	autograph
bi-	two	bicycle
co-	equal, together	co-operate
contra-	opposite	contradict
counter-	against	counteract
de-	making the opposite of	demist
dis-	not, opposite of	disobey
dis-	undoing, making opposite	disconnect
ex-	used to be	ex-soldier
ex-	out of	extract
fore-	in the front of	foreground
fore-	before	foretell
hyper-	very big	hypermarket
in-	not, opposite of	incorrect
in-	in, into	insight
inter-	between	international
mal-	bad	malfunction
mini-	small	mini-computer
mis-	wrong, false	mistake
mono-	one	monochrome

Prefix	Meaning	Examples
multi-	many	multi-purpose
neo-	new	neo-fascist
non-	not, opposite of	non-smoker
out-	beyond	outlaw
over-	too much	overdone
poly-	many	polyhedron
post-	after	postpone
pre-	before	premature
pro-	for	pro-British
re-	again	reprocess
re-	back	reverse
semi-	half	semiconscious
sub-	below	submarine
sub-	less than	substandard
super-	more than, special	superman
sur-	more than, beyond	surpass
trans-	across	transport
tri-	three	tricycle
ultra-	beyond	ultraviolet
ultra-	very much indeed	ultra-rich
un-	not, opposite of	unfair
un-	making opposite	undo
under-	below, less than	underpass
uni-	one	unicycle

Making plurals

Plural means 'more than one'.
Most words follow these rules:

1 Normally, just add **-s**.

book	→	book**s**
complication	→	complication**s**

2 Words that end in **-s**, add **-es**.

glass	→	glass**es**
genius	→	genius**es**

3 Words that end in **-x** and **-z**, add **-es**.

box	→	box**es**
buzz	→	buzz**es**

4 Words that end in **-ch** and **-sh**, add **-es**.

branch	→	branch**es**
bush	→	bush**es**

5 Words that end in **-f** or **-fe**, change the ending to **-ve** and add **-s**.

calf	→	cal**ves**
wife	→	wi**ves**

Exceptions

beliefs	chiefs	dwarfs	griefs
gulfs	proofs	roofs	

6 Words that end in **-y**: if the letter before the **y** is a vowel, just add **-s**.

day	→	day**s**
boy	→	boy**s**

If the letter before the **y** is a consonant, change the **y** to **-ies**.

baby	→	bab**ies**
spy	→	sp**ies**

7 Words that end in **-o**: usually just need an **-s**.

piano	→	piano**s**

Exceptions

A few words add **-es**.

buffalo**es**	mango**es**
cargo**es**	mosquito**es**
domino**es**	motto**es**
echo**es**	potato**es**
go**es**	tomato**es**
grotto**es**	tornado**es**
halo**es**	torpedo**es**
hero**es**	volcano**es**

8 Words that stay the same in the plural:

aircraft	deer	sheep

9 Words that change in a different way:

child	→	children
man	→	men
foot	→	feet
goose	→	geese
mouse	→	mice
tooth	→	teeth
woman	→	women

10 Some Latin and Greek words change in a different way:

crisis	→	crises
formula	→	formulae

Adding -ing and -ed

When we use verbs we have to change them according to the sentence they are in:

> I like to **walk** to school. I **walked** to school yesterday, and I am **walking** to school now.

1 Normally you just add **-ing** and **-ed**.

The rules that follow describe the main exceptions.

2 Words with one syllable, with a long vowel, ending in **-e**. Remove the **-e** and add **-ed** and **-ing**.

rake	rake**d**	rak**ing**
dare	dar**ed**	dar**ing**

But note:		
age	ag**ed**	age**ing**
queue	queue**d**	queue**ing**

3 Words with one syllable, with a short vowel, ending in a single consonant. Double the consonant and add **-ed** and **-ing**.

tap	tapp**ed**	tapp**ing**
beg	begg**ed**	begg**ing**

4 Words with more than one syllable, ending in a single consonant. If the stress is on the last syllable, double the consonant.

propel	propel**led**	propel**ling**

If the stress is not on the last syllable, just add **-ed** and **-ing**.

benefit	benefit**ed**	benefit**ing**
budget	budget**ed**	budget**ing**
sharpen	sharpen**ed**	sharpen**ing**

5 Words ending in **-l**.
If there is only a single vowel before the **l**, add **-led** and **-ling**:

compel	compel**led**	compel**ling**

If there is a double vowel before the **l**, just add **-ed** and **-ing**:

coil	coil**ed**	coil**ing**
peel	peel**ed**	peel**ing**

6 Words ending in **-y**.
If the letter before the **y** is a vowel, just add **-ed** and **-ing**.

play	play**ed**	play**ing**

Exceptions		
lay	→	la**id**
pay	→	pa**id**
say	→	sa**id**

If the letter before the **y** is a consonant, change the **y** to an **i** before adding **-ed**.

cry	cr**ied**	cry**ing**

Adding -ly

We can turn adjectives into adverbs by adding **-ly**:

> He is a quick worker: he works quick**ly**.

Usually you just add **-ly** to the adjective, but there are some exceptions.

1 If the word ends **-ll**, just add **-y**.

> full → ful**ly**

2 If a word of two or more syllables ends in **-y**, cut off the y and add **-ily**.

> happy → happ**ily**

3 One syllable words ending in **-y** are usually regular.

> shy → shy**ly**
>
> **Exceptions**
>
> gay → gaily
> day → daily

4 If the word ends in **-le**, cut off the **e** and add **-y**:

> simple → simp**ly**

Using ie/ei

The rule is: '**i** before **e** except after **c**, when the sound is long ee.'

> th**ie**f   rec**ei**ve
> p**ie**ce   c**ei**ling
>
> **Exceptions**
>
> s**ei**ze   w**ei**r   w**ei**rd

Using -ce/-se

The rule is '**c** for a noun and **s** for a verb.'
(Easy to remember because the letters are in alphabetical order: **C** Noun **S** Verb)

noun	**verb**
advi**ce**	advi**se**
practi**ce**	practi**se**
licen**ce**	licen**se**

> **Example**
>
> I need your advi**ce**: will you advi**se** me?

Words that are easily confused

accept	except	
affect	effect	
aloud	allowed	
bail	bale	
bear	bare	
birth	berth	
board	bored	
chose	choose	
diary	dairy	
great	grate	
heel	heal	
here	hear	
lose	loose	
made	maid	
meter	metre	
miner	minor	
new	knew	
no	know	
pain	pane	
pair	pear	pare
past	passed	past
peace	piece	
quite	quiet	
read	reed	
red	read	
right	write	
sew	sow	
some	sum	
stationary	stationery	
steak	stake	
tale	tail	
there	their	they're
threw	through	
to	two	too
wait	weight	
weak	week	
weather	whether	wether
where	wear	
were	we're	
which	witch	
whose	who's	
wood	would	
your	you're	

Single and double letters

A common spelling problem concerns words with single and/or double letters. Here is a list of the commonest:

accelerate	imitate
address	immediate
assist	marvel
harass	mattress
beginning	millionaire
brilliant	necessary
caterpillar	occasion
collapse	parallel
collect	patrol
commit	pedal
corridor	possess
disappear	sheriff
discuss	success
embarrass	sufficient
exaggerate	terrible
happiness	unnccccssary
illustrate	woollen

Other problem words

adaptation (not adaption)
adviser
computer
conjuror
connection
conqueror
conscience
conscious
encyclopaedia
forty
grandad
granddaughter
miniature
moustache
rhyme
rhythm
somersault
wagon
yoghurt

187

Useful words

accent   the way in which a person pronounces words is described as their accent. Everybody speaks with some kind of accent. If the accent belongs to a particular part of the country, it is called a regional accent. People sometimes talk about a 'posh' or 'BBC' accent. This is correctly called 'received **pronunciation**'. Accent is different from **dialect**.

adjective   adjectives work with **nouns**. They help to make the meaning of the noun clearer or fuller. In these examples the adjectives are *marked out*:
>   I like reading *exciting* books.
>   I'm looking for an *old, green, rusty* bicycle.
>   Peter is very *happy* today.

adverb   adverbs work with **verbs, adjectives** or other adverbs. They help to make their meaning clearer or fuller.
>   *Working with verbs:*
>   He walked *slowly* down the road.
>   *Working with adjectives:*
>   I am feeling *extremely* happy today.
>   *Working with other adverbs:*
>   The car came towards her *agonizingly* slowly.

affix   a part of the word that comes before or after the **stem** or main part. There are two kinds of affix: **prefixes** that come at the beginning of a word, and **suffixes** that come at the end.

apostrophe   see page 180.

argue   to put across a point of view, explaining the reasons why you hold it. For example, 'She argued that the new school uniform was a great improvement on the old, because it was more in line with today's fashions.'

article   the words *a, an, the*.

autobiography   a **biography** that someone writes about themselves.

biography   the story of a person's life.

borrowing   see **loan word**.

casual (language)   when we are speaking to (or writing to) people we know well, we use **vocabulary** and **grammar** that are less **formal** than when we are speaking to people we do not know well. For example we might say to a friend, 'Hang on a bit', while to a stranger we would say, 'Wait a minute'.

clause   a group of words that contains a complete **verb** and makes sense. These are examples of clauses. (The verb is marked in each one):
>   I *hate* coffee ice cream.
>   As I *was going* up the stair,
>   I *met* a man
>   who *was*n't there.

colloquial   conversational language is described as colloquial. It is usually less **formal** than written language.

colon   the punctuation mark **:** . It is used to introduce a list, a saying, or a statement.
>   'We only have one rule in this school: treat others as you would like them to treat you.'

comma   see page 176.

command   see **sentence types**.

conjunction   conjunctions are words that join other words together. In particular they join **phrases** and **clauses**:
>   I like walking along the beach *and* eating ice cream.
>   I only saw the bomb *when* I was nearly on top of it.

dialect   the form of a language used in a particular area (regional, local dialect) or by a particular group of people (social dialect). Different dialects use different **vocabulary** and **grammar**. See page 126.

exclamation   see **sentence types**.

exclamation mark   see page 175.

first (language)   the language that we are brought up to speak at home. It is sometimes called the mother tongue. For most in Britain this is English, but many have a different first language: for example Gujarati, or Turkish.

formal (language)   when we are speaking to (or writing to) people whom we do not know well, we use language that is formal. We pay more careful attention to the **grammar** of our sentences and we use **vocabulary** that we know anyone will find acceptable. See **casual**.

full stop   see page 175.

genre   a form of writing, especially fiction, that is readily identified. For example: romance, detective story, science fiction. (See page 148.)

gesture   when we speak to other people we often use movements of our bodies, especially of our hands and arms, to help communicate our meaning. These movements are called gestures.

grammar   grammar tells us how the words of a language are combined to make sentences. In English this is done by *word order* and *changing the form of words*:
> *word order:* 'I saw Peter yesterday.' is an English sentence. 'Yesterday saw Peter I.' isn't.
> *changing the form of words:* the verb 'see' changes to 'saw'. We say 'I saw Peter yesterday.' and not 'I see Peter yesterday.'

image/imagery   people often describe things in speech or writing by comparing them with something else. This helps to make their meaning clearer or more vivid:
> *He's not athletic; he's a real couch potato.*
This doesn't, of course, mean that the person is literally a potato. It focuses our attention on particular things about a potato and so tells us something about the person. Potatoes don't do anything or move about – they just stay in the same place underground and slowly get bigger. The person described doesn't do anything or move about; he stays in the same place (in this case the couch) and slowly gets bigger, through inactivity and overeating, while watching TV. (See **metaphor** and **simile**.)

inverted comma   see page 179.

loan word   a word which is borrowed from another language. In English café is a borrowing from French, bungalow is a borrowing from Gujarati.

media   short for *mass media* or *communication*: the ways in which people can communicate with large audiences: newspapers, magazines, radio and TV, for example. *Media* is a plural: one *medium*, several *media*.

metaphor   an **image** that involves comparing two things, without spelling out that a comparison is being made:
> The car *scorched* into the driveway.
> Mary is a real *camel* in games lessons.
(See **image** and **simile**.)

metre   in **verse** a regular pattern of strong and weak syllables:
> Was this the face that launched a thousand ships?
This line has a regular pattern of weak STRONG weak STRONG and so on. Therefore it is *metrical*.

narrative   writing or talking that tells the story of something that happened. A narrative may be true, or it may be fiction.

narrator   the person who tells the narrative.

non-standard   using **vocabulary** or **grammar** in ways that are not correct for **Standard English**.

noun   nouns are words that refer to people, places, things and ideas: cake, thought, child, sand, butter, happiness, November.

object   in **statement** sentences, the object normally comes after the **verb**. It refers to the person or thing that is affected by the action of the verb:
> The dog bit *the postman.*
> I've lost *the notebook with my maths homework in it.*

phrase   a group of words that makes sense, but not full sense on its own. A phrase does not contain a complete verb. Examples:
> coffee ice cream
> playing football
> the biggest aspidistra in the world
See **clause**.

plot the main events in a story and the way in which they are linked together.

point of view when something happens it can be reported in different ways according to who is telling the story. For example if Mark and Imran have a row, Mark's version of what happened will be different from Imran's. If we are making up a story, we can choose to tell it from different points of view.

prefix an affix that comes at the beginning of a word. In the words *preposition*, *prefix* and *preparation*, the prefix is *pre-*.

preposition prepositions come before **nouns** and **adverbs**. They are the 'little words' of English:
up the hill, *by* now, *for* example, *until* then.

pronoun pronouns are used to stand instead of **nouns**. They help us to avoid too much repetition. Some of the commonest pronouns are:
I, she, he, you, we, they, it,
me, her, him, us, them,
my, his, our, your, their, its,
myself, himself, herself, ourselves,
yourselves, themselves, itself,
who, whom, whose, that, what, which,
this, that, these, those.

pronunciation the way in which a person speaks the words of a language.

proof-reading reading through something that someone has written and correcting all the mistakes of spelling, punctuation and grammar.

prose writing in ordinary sentences. Prose is different from **verse** or poetry.

pun a play on words. Often words have more than one meaning (or two different words are pronounced in the same way) and we can make jokes by playing with these meanings. 'Knock knock' jokes often use puns:
Knock knock
Who's there?
Rice Crispies
Rice Crispies who?
I'll tell you next week, it's a cereal.

purpose how we write or speak is affected by the audience and the purpose we have: why we are writing or speaking to them and the effect we want to have on them.

question see **sentence types**.

question mark see page 175.

report a **narrative** that sets out in a straightforward way what happened. (It also has a special meaning in the phrase 'school report'!)

rhyme when two words end with a similar sound pattern, they rhyme: for example sit/hit, house/grouse, examination/complication. Rhyme is often used in poetry.

rhythm the pattern of strong and weak beats in speech or writing. Rhythm is important in poetry, but it can be important in **prose**, too.

root another word for **stem**.

second (language) some countries have several different first languages. So that people with different first languages can talk to each other, they have to learn a common second language. (For example, in India Hindi or English is many people's second language. In Britain people who do not have English as their first language usually have it as their second language.)

semi-colon see page 177.

sentence types there are four main types of sentence:
Statement: This is a statement.
Question: What is the question?
Command: Give me a command.
Exclamation: What a wonderful idea that was!

setting the time and place where a story happens.

simile an **image** that involves comparing two things and makes it obvious that a comparison is being made:
Your explanation is *as clear as mud.*
(See **image** and **metaphor**.)

slang casual language that is special to one group of people. (Examples of this are school slang, thieves' slang, motorbike slang.) It is often not acceptable outside that group. If you use slang outside the proper group you may well be criticized or laughed at.

Standard English   the **dialect** of English that is used when speaking in formal situations, and normally in writing.

statement   see **sentence types**.

stem   the main part of a word, to which **prefixes** and **suffixes** can be added. In the words *superman* and *manly* the stem is *man*. (See page 182.)

subject   the subject of a sentence tells us what it is about. In a statement sentence it comes at the beginning:

    Miriam is unhappy.
    The big blue book on the table is mine.

suffix   an **affix** that comes at the end of the word. In the words *manly* and *slowly*, the suffix is *-ly*. (See page 182.)

syllable   words can be made up of one or more syllables. Roughly speaking you can work out how many syllables a word has by counting the number of 'beats' as you say it:

    1 syllable – bat, school, bounced
    2 syllables – batted, bouncing
    3 syllables – unbuttoned, Barnstaple

typeface   the different form that letters can have in a printed book. These are examples of different typefaces:

    typeface   typeface   typeface

verb   it is difficult to write a proper sentence without a complete verb. Most verbs will fit into one or more of these spaces:

    He —————— it. (eg *liked*)
    She ——————. (eg *is singing*)
    It ————— good. (eg *is*)

verse   writing that uses **rhyme** and/or **rhythm**.

vocabulary   the words of a language, or a piece of speech or writing.

Acknowledgements

The editors and publisher are grateful for permission to reprint the following copyright material:

John Agard: from *Mangoes and Bullets* (Pluto Press, 1985). Reprinted by kind permission of John Agard c/o Caroline Sheldon Literary Agency. **Michael Anthony:** 'Enchanted alley' published in *Best West Indian Stories* (Nelson, 1982). Reprinted by permission of Andre Deutsch Ltd. **Peter Appleton:** 'The other time' published in *Standpoints*, ed. John Foster (Nelson). **Steve Barlow and Steve Skidmore:** first published in this collection, by permission of the authors. © Steve Barlow and Steve Skidmore 1991. **James Berry:** 'The banana tree' from *A Thief in the Village* (Hamish Hamilton Children's Books, 1987), © James Berry 1987. Reprinted by permission of Hamish Hamilton Ltd. 'Freedom' from *Bluefoot Traveller*, ed. James Berry (1985). Reprinted by permission of Thomas Nelson & Sons Ltd. **Alan Bold:** 'Mary Cummings', first published in *A Fourth Poetry Book* (Oxford University Press). © Alan Bold 1982. Reprinted by permission of the author. **Patrick Boyle:** from *At Night All Cats Are Grey* (McGibbon & Kee). © Patrick Boyle 1966. **Geoffrey Chaucer:** from *The General Prologue to the Canterbury Tales*, ed. James Winny, and from *The Pardoner's Prologue and Tale*, ed. A.C. Spearing. Reprinted by permission of Cambridge University Press. **Wendy Cope:** 'Sisters', reprinted by permission of the author. **Peter Dunn:** 'The suit' (originally entitled 'Sir Cyril to enter the Palace in jaunty style') from *The Independent*, 14 September 1988. Used with permission. **David Eddings:** from *The Castle of Wizardry* © David Eddings 1984. Published by Corgi Books. All rights reserved. **Robert Graves:** from *Collected Poems* (1975). Reprinted by permission of A. P. Watt Ltd on behalf of the Trustees of the Robert Graves Copyright Trust. **Graham Greene:** from *Collected Stories* (William Heinemann Ltd/The Bodley Head Ltd). Reprinted by permission of Laurence Pollinger Ltd. **Woodie Guthrie:** 'Pretty Boy Floyd' © 1961 Fall River Music Inc, assigned to Harmony Music Ltd, 1a Farm Place, London, W8 7SX for the UK & Eire. Used with permission. **David Harmer, Ian McMillan, and Martyn Wiley:** from *Overstone* (1988). Reprinted by permission of Thomas Nelson & Sons Ltd. **Raymond Harris:** from *The Broken Worlds* (Headline) © Raymond Harris 1986. Reprinted by permission of David Grossman Literary Agency Ltd. **Gwen Harwood:** from *Selected Poems*, © Gwen Harwood. Reprinted by permission of Collins/Angus & Robertson Publishers, Australia. **Robert Ingpen:** from *The Idle Bear* (1986), © Robert Ingpen 1986. First published by Lothian Publishing Company Pty, Melbourne, Australia. **Barbara Jacobs:** from *Not Really Working*, © Barbara Jacobs 1990. Published by Corgi Freeway. All rights reserved. **Dean R. Koontz:** from *The Mask*, © 1981 Nkui Inc. Reprinted by permission of Headline Book Publishing PLC. **Gavin Lyall:** from *Midnight Plus One*, front cover reproduced by permission of Hodder & Stoughton Publishers; text reprinted by permission of Peters Fraser & Dunlop Group Ltd. **Aidan Macfarlane and Anne McPherson:**

Acknowledgements

from *Diary of a Teenage Health Freak* (OUP, 1987). Reprinted by permission of Oxford University Press. **Lensey Namioka:** from *Visions* edited by Donald R. Gallo. Reprinted by permission of Ruth Cohen Inc, Literary Agent. **Alma Norman:** from *Ballads of Jamaica*, edited by A. Norman (Longman, 1967). Reprinted by permission of Longman Group UK. **Sean O'Neill:** from *The Indy*, 31 September 1989. Reprinted by permission of Young Newspaper Publishing Ltd. **Brian Patten:** 'The newcomer' © Brian Patten from *Gargling with Jelly* (Viking Kestrel, 1985). Reprinted by permission of Rogers Coleridge & White Ltd on behalf of the author. **Gloria Rawlinson:** from *For Today and Tomorrow* ed. H. Sergeant. Reprinted by permission of Evans Brothers/Unwin Hyman, part of HarperCollins Publishers. **Dr Peter Rowan:** from *Can You Get Warts from Touching Toads?* Reprinted by permission of the publisher Jonathan Cape Ltd on behalf of the author. **Christopher Rush:** 'My grandmother' (poem) from *A Resurrection of a Kind* and prose extract from *A Twelvemonth and a Day*. Reprinted by permission of the Aberdeen University Press Ltd (Publishers). **Albie Sachs:** from *The Jail Diary of Albie Sachs* (Harvill Press, 1966) © Albie Sachs 1966. Reprinted by permission of Tessa Sayle Agency. **Mohamad Haji Salleh:** from *For Today and Tomorrow*, ed. H. Sergeant. Reprinted by permission of Evans Brothers/Unwin Hyman, part of HarperCollins Publishers. **William Saroyan:** from *Dear Baby* (Faber). Reprinted by permission of Laurence Pollinger Ltd. **Carole Senior:** 'Blackbird', © Carole Senior 1991. Reprinted by permission of the author. **Stevie Smith:** from *The Collected Poems of Stevie Smith* (Penguin 20th Century Classics). Reprinted by permission of James MacGibbon, Literary Executor. **Will Stanton:** 'Barney' published in *Story Lines* ed. A. Thompson (1971). Reprinted by permission of the author. **Terry Tapp:** 'That's show biz!' published in *Space 6*, ed. Richard Davis (Hutchinson).

We should like to thank Owen Davies, for the drafts of *Revenge is Sweet*, staff and pupils at Reddish Vale School, Stockport, and staff at the Hereford County Hospital. We are also grateful for permission to include the two extracts from school uniform regulations.

Although every effort has been made to trace and contact copyright holders before publication, we have not been successful in a few cases. If notified, the publishers will be pleased to rectify any omissions at the earliest opportunity.

The illustrations are by:
Susan André p86/87; **Tony Ansell** p120, p121, p123, p124; **John Bendall-Brunello** p142/143; **Grahame McKay Black** p70/71, p74/75, p77, p78, p92; **Tony James Chance** p24, p25, p81, p83, p84, pp156-163; **Martin Chatterton** pp164-170; **Colin T. Clifton** p136, p137; **Gerard Gibson** p8, p91, p101; **Robin Harris** p17, p21, p22; **Michael Hingley** p29; **Linda Jeffrey** pp106-111; **Diane Lumley** p69; **Nilesh Mistry** p32/33; **Mike Nicholson** p95, p96, p97, p146, p147; **Oxford Illustrators Ltd** p119, p141; **Fiona Powers** p10/11; **Michael Reid** p30/31; **Julie Roberts** p14, p116, p117; **Michael Sheehy** p44, p98; **Duncan Storr** p34, p37, p39; **Lee Sullivan** p60, p62, p65; **Martin Ursell** p26, p27, p50/51, p52, p54, p56; **Jolyon Webb** p57, p58. The handwriting is mainly by Elitta Fell.

The publishers would like to thank the following for permission to reproduce photographs:
Heather Angel p46; **British Canoe Union** p133 (upper middle left); **Martyn F. Chillmaid** p6 (top), p7 (top), p24 (top); **Bruce Coleman Ltd** p47; **Mary Evans Picture Library** p7 (right); **Express Newspapers plc** p43 (right); **Sally & Richard Greenhill** p6 (left), p7 (bottom), p133 (bottom left); **Asadour Guzelian** p138; **Impact Photos/Mark Cator** p133 (lower middle left), **Impact Photos/Piers Cavendish** p133 (lower middle right), **Impact Photos/John Cole** p133 (top right); **Impact Photos/Alain Le Garsmeur** p133 (bottom right); **London Features International Ltd/Neal Preston** p133 (upper middle right); **Magnum Photos Ltd/Elliott Erwitt** p43 (top); **Metropolitan Police Office** p133 (top left); **Robert Musson** p6 (bottom); **National Anti-Vivisection Society Ltd** p42 (left); **Punch Publications Ltd** p42 (top and bottom), p43 (left); **John Seely** p112 (all), p113 (both), p114 (all), p115, pp127-131 (all), p134, p135; **Severn Trent Water Ltd** p24 (bottom); **Robert Taylor** p126; **United Feature Syndicate, Inc.** p68.

The cover photograph is reproduced by permission of Manfred Kage/Science Photo Library.

A CIP catalogue record for this book is available from the British Library.

Oxford University Press, Walton Street, Oxford OX2 6DP

Oxford   New York   Toronto
Delhi   Bombay   Calcutta   Madras   Karachi
Petaling Jaya   Singapore   Hong Kong   Tokyo
Nairobi   Dar es Salaam   Cape Town
Melbourne   Auckland

and associated companies in
Berlin   Ibadan

Oxford is a trademark of Oxford University Press

© John Seely, Frank Green, and David Kitchen 1991
First published 1991
Reprinted 1992

ISBN 0 19 831163 X

Printed in Italy